D0125999

Living with a Labrador Retriever

Edited by Jo Coulson

First edition for the United States and Canada published
2000 by Barron's Educational Series, Inc.

All inquiries should be addressed to:

Barron's Educational Series, Inc.
250 Wireless Boulevard
Hauppauge, NY 11788
http://www.barronseduc.com

International Standard Book Number: 0-7641-5260-2

Library of Congress Catalog Card No: 00-103184

Printed in Singapore

9 8 7 6 5

CONTENTS

CHAPTER ONE

HISTORY OF THE LABRADOR RETRIEVER

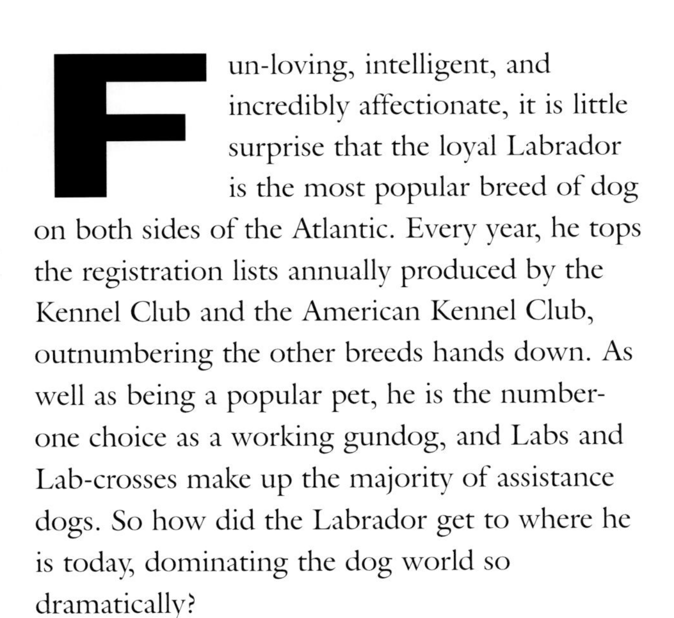

Fun-loving, intelligent, and incredibly affectionate, it is little surprise that the loyal Labrador is the most popular breed of dog on both sides of the Atlantic. Every year, he tops the registration lists annually produced by the Kennel Club and the American Kennel Club, outnumbering the other breeds hands down. As well as being a popular pet, he is the number-one choice as a working gundog, and Labs and Lab-crosses make up the majority of assistance dogs. So how did the Labrador get to where he is today, dominating the dog world so dramatically?

Humble Beginnings

Although the details of the Labrador's history are much disputed by dog historians, the key points of the breed's history are well documented. He first came to the attention of European fishermen working on the west coast of Canada in the Newfoundland and St. John's areas. These fishermen used local dogs who were fantastic workers—bringing in heavy nets, retrieving any fish that had fallen overboard into the cold, icy water, and even fetching wood to smoke the fish once they were brought on land.

In return, the fishermen fed the dogs any fish scraps. Some authorities claim the dogs were fed only in winter, and that they were left to hunt for themselves in the summer. If the dogs were always wondering where the next meal would come from, this could well explain the origins of the Labrador's constant search for food!

The dogs were called Newfoundlands or St. John's dogs, named after the area where they were found. It seems there were two types of fishing dogs in the area: the first a large, heavy-coated type that was called the Newfoundland; the second, a smaller smooth-coated type called the St. John's dog or Lesser Newfoundland, appears to be the forerunner of the modern-day Labrador.

PORTUGUESE ORIGINS?

How the Newfoundland or St. John's dogs came to be in Canada is open to much debate. It is unlikely that the dogs descend from native Indian dogs in the area, nor from any dogs that the Vikings brought over.

The strongest theory posited is that Portuguese traders and fishermen are likely to have introduced their water dogs to the area as early as 1500.

Influential breeder Mary Roslin-Williams first brought attention to the similarity between the Portuguese Water Dog and the Labrador Retriever, and the Portuguese language offers further clues. *Lavrador* translates as "labourer," and the Portuguese Cattle Dog (closely related to the Water Dog) is called *Cane di Castro Laboreiro*.

Arriving in Britain

English fishermen brought some of the dogs back with them, and the story is that they swam ashore from the boats as they landed in Poole Harbour in Dorset. There, they caught the attention of the second Earl of Malmesbury at the beginning of the 19th century. When he saw the dogs scavenging in and around the water for any discarded fish, the Earl recognized their retrieving talents, and bought four for his estate at Hurn Court, in Dorset.

Legend has it that the first Labrador Retrievers to arrive in England swam ashore from fishing boats.

The dogs' water retrieving skills were of particular interest to the Earl, since the Hurn estate had many wildfowl, and a dog was needed to retrieve birds quickly that were shot and fell into the water.

Other landed gentry became interested in these new retrievers, and so the breed grew. This, thankfully, saved the Labrador from possible extinction in its homeland. In 1885, the government made moves to promote sheep breeding in the Newfoundland area, which meant discouraging the keeping and breeding of dogs by imposing punitive taxes. At the same time, quarantine was introduced in Britain, making it very difficult to import dogs.

Fortunately, a good foundation for the breed had already been established, particularly in England and Scotland. The third Earl of Malmesbury had the same enthusiasm for the breed as his ancestor, and imported many more dogs. The Duke of Buccleuch and the eleventh Earl of Home were two other notable guardians of the breed.

The Labrador's wonderful sense of smell, combined with its retrieving ability, made the breed invaluable in the field.

The Labrador gradually became increasingly popular with the aristocracy, and offspring of outstanding dogs were given as gifts to other estates.

Changes in the Field

The second half of the 19th century was a crucial time for the development of the gundog breeds. The change from the muzzle-loading gun to the faster breech-loading gun meant more birds could be shot—and at a faster rate, so a faster bird-dog was needed to retrieve the fallen prey.

Although the Labrador was suitable for this type of work, it was actually the Flat Coated Retriever that became popular in the field during this time. The Labrador's huge rise to popularity was yet to come. The reason why the Labrador was to supersede the Flat Coat and become the supreme retriever was his wonderful nose—Labradors work on ground scent, while Flat Coats tend to work more on airborne scent.

Retriever Breeds

It was not until 1903 that the Kennel Club recognized the Labrador as a separate variety of retriever. It was another 13 years before the Labrador Retriever Club was established with the aim of keeping the breed as pure as possible. Before this date, puppies were classed according to which retriever breed they most resembled; sometimes puppies in the same litter could be categorized as different breeds altogether.

The Club's first chairman was the Hon. Arthur Holland-Hibbert (later Lord Knutsford), who had also been instrumental in persuading the Kennel Club to give official recognition to the Labrador as a breed. As well as drawing up the first Breed Standard (which remained unchanged until 1950), the Club also organized and supported Field Trial events.

Dual Purpose

Holland-Hibbert's Munden Single was the first Labrador to be entered at a Field Trial, back in

Strenuous efforts have been made to keep the Labrador's working heritage alive.

1904, where she was awarded a Certificate of Merit. She won at shows in 1903, 1904, and 1905. In 1904 she won the first Challenge Certificate (CC) ever awarded to a Labrador bitch. In 1905 she won first prize in the Field Trials Class at Crufts.

She was a highly prized working dog, and was considered such an excellent example of her breed that, when she died in 1909, she was preserved and exhibited in the British Museum, until moved to the Walter Rothschild Zoological Museum in Tring, Hertfordshire, shortly after World War II.

Throughout the breed's history, enthusiasts have worked to keep its heritage as a gundog and retriever alive. Even today in the U.K., a Labrador cannot earn the full title of Champion unless he has a working certificate as well as three Challenge Certificates. However, despite the best intentions of avoiding a show/working split in the breed, there have only ever been ten dual Champions. The first was Banchory Bolo in 1923, and the last, Knaith Banjo, was whelped in 1946. Banjo was one of just two yellow Labs to become dual Champions—the other being Staindrop Saighdear, born in 1944. The remaining seven were all black Labs.

To America

The growth of the Labrador took a very similar course in the United States. The American Kennel Club registered its first Labrador—a bitch import from Scotland called Brocklehirst Nell—in 1917. It didn't take long before the

Labrador's popularity with the more affluent classes took off, and, in the 1920s, several rich American families imported Labradors and accompanying gamekeepers (most of them Scottish) for their estates.

Several kennels worked to improve the breed, but progress was disrupted by World War II. After the war, as in the U.K., dog showing became more popular, and soon the benches were graced not only with kennel owners, but also some pet owners proud to show off their prized purebred dogs.

Pedigree dog ownership was becoming more popular, and the Labrador, with his wonderful temperament, became a firm favorite—a position he has kept to the present day.

Colors

At the start of the breed's development, the Labrador was always considered a black dog (though then, as now, some dogs sported a white spot on their chest). Other colors did emerge in litters, but they were rarely bred from, and they were not indicative of what was commonly accepted as a Labrador.

Colonel Radclyffe, an influential enthusiast of the breed, was the first to register a yellow Labrador—Ben of Hyde. He traces back to Radclyffe's Turk, a direct import from Newfoundland in 1871. Veronica Wormald founded the Yellow Labrador Retriever Club in 1924, producing a separate (though unofficial) Breed Standard for the yellows.

Originally, the Labrador was always a black dog.

The yellow Labrador is a popular choice.

The chocolate Labrador underwent a similar struggle to be recognized on the same terms as the black Labrador. It is reported that the Buccleuch estate in Dalkeith, Scotland, had two chocolate puppies in the 1890s. The first chocolate Champion was not seen in the U.K. until the bitch, Ch. Cookridge Tango, was born in 1961 (becoming a Champion in 1964). The first U.S. chocolate Champion was Ch. Invails Pogey Bait, in the late 1950s. As with the yellow strain, it was the discovery that a few leading dogs carried the chocolate gene that gave the new color more credibility, and led to its acceptance as a valid Labrador color.

Most people have their own color preference, and breeders rarely have all three varieties. People who work their dogs almost exclusively prefer black Labs; the yellow is particularly popular with pet people; and the chocolate, although more unusual, has a loyal fan-base too.

Chocolates had a struggle for recognition.

The People's Choice

The breed remained a well-kept secret of the upper-class shooting fraternity until around the mid-1950s, a time when people had recovered from the hardship of the war, and society generally was more affluent and had more leisure time. The showing of pedigree dogs became increasingly popular as a pastime, and this helped to bring the breed to the attention of more people. By the late 1950s, with the Kennel Club introduction of the Show Champion title, the Labrador was no longer considered the preserve of the hunting, shooting, fishing world, and it soon became the most popular pedigree dog to own.

The Labrador's easygoing, friendly temperament makes him a popular choice for a family dog, and his adaptable nature means that, provided all his exercise needs are met, he will be as much at home in a twenty-bedroom mansion in the Scottish Highlands as he is in a one-bedroom house in the city.

The Labrador loves being busy, and, just as he helped fishermen 200 years ago, so he will try to be useful around the house—whether that involves bringing in the morning paper or fetching your slippers. Your Labrador will love sharing his life with you and will do everything to show his devotion. It is this loyal, loving character that has assured the breed's current success—and means that he will probably remain the most popular pedigree dog for the next 200 years.

The Labrador is now rated as the most popular of pedigree dogs.

CHAPTER TWO

PUPPY POWER

Living with a Labrador puppy is a sheer joy—your house will be full of cuddles, smiles, and laughter, and after just a few days you will wonder how you ever lived without him.

However, there is another side. Raising a pup is hard work. It can be compared to looking after a baby—although puppies are far more mobile and seem to get themselves into more trouble. Who has ever found their eight-week-old baby chewing electrical wires or scaling their sideboard to smash a family treasure, previously considered safely out of reach?

If you have never experienced puppyhood before—or if you have forgotten what it was *really* like—let us refresh your memory...

Should You Have a Dog?

First things first—are you really sure you can look after a Labrador for the next 12 years or so? Ask yourself the following questions.

- Are you really prepared to give your Labrador two walks a day, every day, in all weather?
- Are you prepared to make arrangements for your dog to be looked after if you go away on vacation?
- Can you be sure that your lifestyle will not change dramatically in the dog's lifetime—for example, that you will not have to take up full-time employment (no dog should be left at home from 9 A.M.–5 P.M.)?
- Can you afford to keep a dog? Not only do you have to pay for his food, his equipment (bed, toys, lead, and collar), his worm and flea treatments, and his vaccinations, you will also have to be prepared to pay costly and sometimes unexpected veterinary bills.
- Is everyone in the family happy to have a pet, and are they prepared to share the responsibility?
- Are you sure that all family members are not allergic to dogs? If you are in any doubt, arrange for the family to spend some time

with an adult dog and monitor any adverse reactions.

Ask yourself why you want a Labrador. It may be simply because you cannot resist the cute, angelic little bundle you have seen in advertisements. If this is the case, then think again. A tiny little pup grows into a hefty adult, which requires constant care.

Do you have the space for a Labrador? If you live in a small apartment, perhaps a smaller breed would suit you better. If you are very neat and will object to stubborn Lab hairs getting all over the carpet and furniture, perhaps you should consider a non-shedding breed—or a goldfish!

Try to see as many different Labradors as possible, so that you can choose the type you prefer.

Read as much as you can on the breed and talk to experienced owners about the real nitty-gritty of sharing your life with a Labrador. Contact your national Kennel Club for details of Labrador breed clubs, and talk to some of their members. Visit a club show—not only will you be able to see lots of Labradors, you will also be able to talk to the owners.

Show or Working Type?

Once you are sure the Labrador is the breed for you, it's time to search for your pup. First, you should decide what type of Lab you prefer. There are two distinct types—the heavier-built "show" Labrador, and the more athletic, working type. If you are someone who is just looking for a family pet, you would be advised to stick to the show type. The working Lab does not have the laid-back attitude needed in a pet home and needs to be employed in an active, gundog environment to be kept fully stimulated.

However, there is considerable choice within the show category—and the more Labs you see, the more you will notice slight differences between various lines. Once you have identified the look you want, ask your breed club if they can recommend anyone suitable. If you have seen a particular type you admire at a show, talk to the breeder, and ask if he or she is planning a litter.

Finding a Good Breeder

When you visit the litter, you should assess the mother's temperament. She should be friendly and confident, with no sign of nervousness or

The mother's temperament will give you an indication of how the puppies will turn out.

aggression. In terms of general appearance, is she a good example of the breed? Do remember that she won't be looking her best, having recently given birth, but you will get an idea of her general health and appearance. The puppies' father may not live nearby for you to inspect him, but you should make inquiries about his temperament and health—and the breeder will probably have a photo so you can see what he looks like.

Health checks are all important. What are the parents' hip scores? What are the elbow scores? Do they have clear eye certificates? Different countries run different tests, so contact your Kennel Club or veterinarian for information on how the tests work and what results you should be looking for. (See pages 126 and 127 for more information.) It is important to research beyond the puppies' parents—the parents could have great scores, but if the grandparents and great-grandparents have a history of bad hips, the pups could be affected too.

At eight weeks, a Labrador puppy should look balanced and in proportion.

A good breeder will ask you many questions too—and may insist on doing a home-check to make sure the puppy will be raised in a suitable and safe environment. References may also be requested (e.g., if you have owned a dog before, the breeder may want a reference from your veterinarian).

Watch the puppies playing together, and you will see their individual personalities emerge.

Inspect where the puppies have been raised. Their living-quarters should be clean and within the breeder's home. Some breeders raise puppies outside in kennels, but this is not ideal. Early socialization is crucial, and your puppy will have a better start in life if he becomes familiar with household sounds and has as much contact with people as possible.

Healthy puppies should look like a box with a leg on each corner. They should stride equally on all four legs (rather than bunny-hopping with their back legs together). The puppies should be clean, should smell nice and fresh, and obviously there shouldn't be any evidence of flea infestation.

Ideal Choice

The sex you choose is a matter of personal preference. There is very little difference between male and female Labs—while some people prefer bitches and others (male) dogs, there are no significant character differences between the two sexes. If you have a dog, be aware of how he develops sexually, and make sure he has no opportunity to wander off (your yard should be fenced securely). Remember also that, when in season, a bitch can become desperate to mate and may also be inclined to wander (see Neutering in Chapter Three).

It is advisable to avoid the shy puppy that is reluctant to come forward. Dealing with nervous puppies is best left to experienced owners. With some breeds, it is not always advisable to pick the most assertive pup as this could indicate a dominant character that could cause problems. However, the Labrador is not generally a dominant breed, and the brazen pup that comes forward to chew your shoelaces should not necessarily be ruled out!

If you intend to buy a show dog, take the advice of the breeder—then keep your fingers crossed! At this stage, you can only evaluate potential; there are no guarantees that a good-looking eight-week-old pup is going to end up a Champion.

Remember that, although a small white spot on the chest is permissible in the show ring, it will grow as the puppy grows. A small spot on an eight-week-old pup will be quite a size on a one-year-old. For more information on show potential, see Chapter Seven, Seeking Perfection.

Colors

Again, the color of your Lab is a matter of personal preference—there are no character differences between the three colors.

Yellow

The yellow color ranges from light cream to red fox—and so there is plenty of scope for choice just within this color. Generally, a puppy's ears will be darker than his body, and this is a good indication of the color he will be as an adult.

Young yellow Labs tend to have a little pink pigmentation, particularly on the nose. Look at the pads to see if darker pigmentation is present, as this is an indication that the pup's pigment color will darken with time. By eight weeks, dark pigmentation should be evident.

Chocolate

How a chocolate Lab develops depends on his individual coloring. Chocolates range from a very light, mink color, to a very dark color (similar to bitter plain chocolate). Most chocolates will darken at 12 weeks when they start losing their puppy fluff, and may give an indication of how the puppy will turn out. If you want a darker-colored chocolate Lab (as preferred in the show ring), avoid a pup with pink pads and look for dark pigmentation of the pads, as well as of the eyelids and nose. Unusually, a chocolate's eyes may darken throughout the dog's life.

You will have to wait until a chocolate is around 12 weeks old before you get an accurate idea of how dark he will be.

Black

The black Lab puppy will be born black and will stay black (though old age may see his muzzle gray slightly). As before, if you plan to show your dog, you may want to avoid one with a noticeable white spot on his chest, as it will grow in size and be undesirable in the show ring. Again, it is a matter of personal choice. Some pet owners are quite proud of their Lab's "medallion" on his chest. A few black

Labs have some white hairs on their pads; these are known as "Bolo pads," after a famous Champion. Whether the white hairs denote the ancestry of Bolo, or whether this is nothing more than an old wives' tale, is open to conjecture.

Preparing for Your Pup

Before you bring your chosen pup home, there are important preparations to make. Look at your home through a puppy's eyes. Lie flat on your stomach on the floor of every room and remove any hazards you see. Then see what the pup can reach—ashtrays on low coffee tables, poisonous houseplants, dried flower arrangements, breakable ornaments; the list is seemingly endless—but it is better to be safe than sorry.

To avoid joint strain, your puppy should not be allowed to tackle the stairs until he has grown. If you don't have a door barring access to the stairs, use a child stair-gate (and train all family members to automatically shut it behind them).

Before bringing the pup home, you should also make sure you have all the equipment you will need.

A cardboard box, lined with bedding, is comfortable—and it doesn't matter if it gets chewed!

Bed

Although he will need a "proper" bed eventually, it is worth adapting a cardboard box for the first few weeks. Whatever bed you make or buy, he will soon chew it to shreds, so a disposable bed that is easily replaced will save you money. A little comfortable bedding (such as absorbent, fleecy veterinary bedding) will make his box a very cozy place to lay his head.

Alternatively, you might like to consider a puppy crate (see page 23).

Bowls

There is a wide range of bowls to choose from. Stainless steel bowls are very sturdy, and will rarely need replacing. Plastic bowls are much cheaper, but they can be chewed easily and are therefore not as durable. Earthenware bowls are popular, but can break. Whatever type of bowl you choose, make sure clean, fresh water is always available, and remove your Lab's food bowl as soon as he has finished eating.

Collar, Tag, and Leash

Buy a soft, light, adjustable puppy collar and a leash. The identification tag bearing your contact details should also be light, so that the pup will hardly notice he is wearing it.

Get the pup used to wearing the collar within a few days of getting him home. (See page 35 for lead-walking.)

Food

The breeder will probably send you home with a puppy pack containing a few days' food, and should also give you a diet sheet outlining what to feed the puppy and when. Find out a few days before taking the pup home what is contained in the diet sheet to ensure you have stocked the right food or ingredients.

Safe Toys

When you are preparing to bring a new pup home, the temptation is to buy every cute toy you can lay your hands on. It is important to provide toys for the pup, but check for quality and durability before parting with your cash. Throw away any toys that are damaged, and always make sure balls are too big to be swallowed by your dog. Every year, hundreds of dogs end up in veterinarians' offices for emergency operations to remove parts of toys that have been chewed and swallowed. Don't let this happen to your precious pup.

Choose toys that are safe and durable.

Beauty Bag

To keep your pup looking beautiful and well manicured, you should buy guillotine-type clippers for your pup's nails, a bristle brush and metal comb for his coat, and a toothbrush and some special doggie toothpaste to keep his smile bright and his breath fresh (see Chapter Four for grooming tips).

Veterinary Appointment

Once you have a date for bringing the pup home, you should contact a veterinarian. If you have not had pets before or are new to the area, ask friends for recommendations. Look up your nearest animal hospitals in the telephone directory and ask if you can visit and chat with one of the veterinarians. Prepare questions before you go, and think about what is really important to you. For example, what medical facilities does the practice have? Does it offer home visits? What are its views on alternative treatments? Your relationship with your Labrador's veterinarian is as important as your relationship with your doctor, and should be built on trust and confidence, so do not rush your decision.

Once you have chosen a veterinary practice, make an appointment for the pup to be seen shortly after you bring him home. The veterinarian can check the pup over and discuss worming and inoculation programs with you (see Chapter Eight). You could also talk to him about microchipping. This is where a tiny microchip (containing a unique number) is inserted between the shoulder blades. The chip can be read with a scanner and will contain the owner's contact details.

Journey Home

The day has finally come to get your pup. Take a friend with you to make the journey home less traumatic—ideally someone who can drive, while you have the puppy on your lap.

Make a little "nest" from a thick towel and put it on your lap. As well as being soft and comfortable, it will also be absorbent in the event of any accidents. Cuddle and reassure him, as it is likely to be the first long journey he has had. Many puppies are carsick on their first trip, but they usually grow out of it as they become more familiar with car travel.

If it is a hot day, make sure the pup is shaded from the sun and that there is adequate ventilation in the car. If you have a long journey, break it up with regular stops so that you can take the puppy out in your arms to enjoy some fresh air. Remember not to put him on the ground or allow him to meet other dogs, since he hasn't had his puppy shots.

At last the time has come to get your puppy.

Getting Pup Home

After all the preparations, it is very exciting to actually get the puppy home. But you—and all the other family members—should try to be calm and relaxed. The pup has been taken from his mother and his siblings, possibly enduring a long car journey, to be thrust into a new home with unfamiliar smells and people: all very daunting when you are just eight weeks old.

First, allow the puppy to go out into the yard, to stretch his legs and relieve himself (see House-Training, page 28). Bring him inside and let him meet the rest of the family, which may also include other pets (see Other Dogs, page 25; Feline Friends, page 25).

All introductions should be calm, so control young children and ask them to be especially gentle with the pup. Too much excitement could overwhelm him. Take it easy for the first few days—you will hopefully have this Labrador for the next 12 years or so, so there's no need to rush anything now.

First Night Nerves

Settle the pup in his bed for the night. Make sure the bed is in a thoroughly safe, puppy-proofed room, checking especially that there are no electrical wires that could be chewed. Make sure the pup can't climb up on any surfaces he could fall from, and keep the windows shut while he is in there unsupervised.

Many people use dog crates, as they offer greater peace of mind (see below).

Doggie Den

Crates are metal cages that can be made into a homey little den with some bedding and a few toys. They should never be used as a punishment cell where you put the pup if he has been naughty. Rather, they should become your Labrador's own little oasis—a place to chew his favorite toy and where he can retreat to if he wants an undisturbed nap.

Unless you plan to replace the crate when your pup grows, it is wise to buy one that will comfortably contain an adult Lab—somewhere in the region of 36 × 24 × 27 inches (90 × 60 × 67.5 cm).

An indoor crate will soon be regarded as a "den" where your puppy can enjoy some peace.

In most cases, a Labrador will learn to love his crate, and will go into it voluntarily if the door is left open. It is also very useful for house-training, as dogs do not like to soil their own sleeping quarters (see House-Training, page 28).

Children

Labradors are renowned for being excellent family dogs, probably because they are such big kids themselves. They love playing games and having fun, and their relationships with children tend to be very close.

However, this is no guarantee that every dog will always behave impeccably with children. Dogs and children should always be supervised, and each should be taught to respect the other and to play gently. Labradors are quite large, and they can be boisterous if they get overexcited. Accidents happen all too easily, and a small child can get knocked over just through overexuberance, so teach your Labrador to behave in a well-mannered way, especially around children.

Children can also get overexcited and so should be taught to be careful around the puppy while he is small. They must understand that, cuddly though he is, the puppy is a living animal—not a toy. Children must also learn to respect the puppy's need for rest. Although a new puppy is hard to resist, he will need lots of sleep, and all family members must be taught to leave him undisturbed.

A puppy must learn to take a treat gently.

Gently

Labs are so enthusiastic about food that they can sometimes snap in their excitement at being given a treat. Teach your Labrador the Gently command from a very young age to stop such bad manners.

- Hold a treat in your hand and offer it to the pup.
- If he takes it gently, say "Gently," praise him and give him the treat.
- If he is at all rough, say "No," and start again.
- When he has mastered the Gently command, allow a child to give a treat under supervision.

Taking Toys

Your children should be taught to respect the dog: not to take his toys, not to disturb him when he is sleeping or eating, never to tease him, and so on. However, in a busy household, it is always difficult to enforce these rules, and your puppy should be taught to be tolerant of children, and not to be possessive about his toys or his food.

- Sit with the puppy and give him a toy. After a short time of him playing with it, take it away from him gently (do not pull hard if he has it in his mouth).
- As soon as you have the toy, give him a treat, lots of praise, and return the toy to him right away. He will realize that he has nothing to lose by letting you have the toy—in fact, he has quite a lot to gain from it!
- If he growls, turn away from him and ignore him. All dogs hate to be ignored, and telling him off is a form of attention that effectively rewards his bad behavior.

Do the same with his food bowl so that he welcomes his bowl being taken away, rather than being possessive of it. Once he is happy with his

A toy must not be grabbed—the pup must wait until it is given to him.

toys and bowl being removed, supervise a child doing the same exercise. If done when he is a puppy, your Lab should grow up thinking it is acceptable for others to touch his things.

It is also worth teaching your Labrador to play with his own toys, and not with toys belonging to children (children should be taught the same in reverse). If you see your Lab with a child's toy, remove it, and give him one of his own.

If you are tactful with your introductions, the resident dog will accept the new arrival as a playmate. Photo courtesy: Anne Taylor.

Other Dogs

Introducing your new pup to any dogs you may already have should be dealt with sensitively. You, of course, will be thrilled to have such an adorable new addition to your family, but your other dogs may not feel the same way.

If your other dogs are Labs, they are likely to welcome the pup—Labs are very sociable, and the pup will be seen as another playmate with which to have fun. In some cases, however, problems can arise, especially if you do not show your dogs that you still love them as much as ever.

Because your pup will not have had his puppy shots, you will have to introduce the dogs in your yard, rather than taking them to neutral territory (such as a nearby park).

Remove all toys in case your dogs object to the pup playing with their possessions, and let them introduce themselves. You will presumably already know that your dogs are good with other canines (otherwise, why did you take on the pup?), so it is really a matter of letting them get to know each other. Even if there is a little growling, try not to interfere. Your pup will understand by your dogs' body language if he is overstepping the mark and should back down. Racing in to rescue the pup is rarely necessary (unless the pup is being physically assaulted) and will only serve to annoy your existing dogs, and make the pup think he is superior to them.

Although raising a pup is a time-consuming business, do make a concerted effort to spend time with your other dogs. Feed them first, let them go through doors before the pup, etc. All these signals will help to show them that, despite the new addition, their positions in the pack are not being threatened.

Feline Friends

Labradors and cats can become great friends. For many cats, the pet Labrador is a great big warm, squashy bed to sleep on (and many Labs

A cat can be surprisingly tolerant—particularly if you control your puppy's initial exuberance.

are more than happy with this arrangement). Of course, when you first bring your pup home, he is likely to be the same size as a cat (sometimes smaller). This may help the cat to accept him more quickly, as he won't be so intimidating. However, puppies are very playful. Unpredictable and overexuberant behavior may not be tolerated by your cat, and she may have to hiss and spit a few times to earn some respect from the pup.

If your Lab really oversteps the mark, the cat may be forced to give a quick swipe of the paw across the nose. Once is usually enough, and they soon come to a mutual understanding. A cat's claws are very sharp and can do serious damage to a pup (especially if she scratches his eyes), so try to prevent their relationship from deteriorating to this level.

Pup Meets Puss

Hold your pup and cuddle him, calling your cat over to you. The curiosity will probably be too much for your cat, and she won't be able to resist investigating further. Talk to them both in a calm, reassuring voice.

Make sure your cat has a high vantage point (such as a shelf) to escape to, safely out of reach of the puppy. Prevent your pup from being too boisterous with her, restraining him gently. The more they get to know each other over a few days, the more you can stop restraining the pup quite as much. As your Lab becomes increasingly familiar with the cat, so will she hold less fascination for him, and they will just go on with their own lives.

One reason why Labradors tend to like cats is that it means more food bowls are put down! To stop your Lab from getting bigger and bigger, and your cat smaller and smaller, make sure you shut your Lab in another room while the cat finishes her meal.

Feeding

If you haven't guessed by now, food is the center of a Lab's life. Even when young, your pup will quickly learn the daytime routine and will soon remind you when it is time for his meal.

Your Lab pup is unlikely to be a fussy eater. However, this is not to say that you should be blasé about what you feed him. It is wise to stick to the diet sheet given to you by the breeder, unless there are very good reasons for changing (perhaps you cannot get hold of the recommended brand, or perhaps it does not agree with your pup). If you do need to change, do so gradually. Put a little of his new food in with his current food. Every day, for the course of 10 days or so, put a little more of the new food in, and take a little more of his current food out. By the end of 10–14 days, a complete changeover should have been achieved.

Mealtimes—the high spot of a Labrador's day.

Do not stray from the diet sheet for the first couple of weeks at least. Change of diet is very stressful to the body, and after being transplanted from one home to another, the last thing your little pup needs is more stress.

Number of Meals

At first, it is likely that your breeder will recommend four (or even five) meals a day. Puppies use up a lot of energy, yet their tummies are very small, so they need to eat little and often. The number of meals is gradually reduced as they get older. With other breeds, you can judge when the meals should be reduced by whether the pup is leaving some of his food; with a Labrador, this is unlikely ever to happen! Follow your breeder's advice, but as a general rule your pup should be on three meals a day by the time he is 12 weeks old, decreasing to two meals a day when he is around six months.

Some owners cut down to one meal a day at around 12 months of age, but it is probably better not to overload the stomach and to split the daily ration into two meals—and your Labrador will certainly appreciate having two high spots in his day!

A puppy needs to be taken out at frequent intervals so that he gets the idea of being clean in the house.

House-Training

This is the part every new puppy owner dreads, but house-training needn't be a headache if you put in the hard work at the beginning. Dogs are very clean animals (despite their love of rolling in cow patties), and hate to soil their own area, so your pup will be very willing to learn.

Take your pup outside to a designated spot in your backyard and tell him to "Hurry up" or "Be clean." As soon as he does his business, praise him handsomely. Reward him with a quick game in the yard before returning inside. If you rush back indoors, he may be less likely to cooperate—realizing that, as soon as he goes to the toilet, the fun in the yard comes to an end.

Take the pup out at the following times.

- First thing in the morning and last thing at night.
- After eating.
- After periods of exercise or excitement (meeting new people, etc.).
- Every two hours.

If you see the pup sniffing the ground (often circling while doing so), call his name in a friendly, excited way, and encourage him out to the backyard. This should stop him in his tracks. As soon as he resumes his business outside, praise him heaps.

Never shout at him for answering a call of nature in an inappropriate place, or he will think that going to the toilet makes you angry, and will avoid doing it in front of you. Then you will find secret puddles all over the house.

Worse still, is shouting at the pup when you come across his "calling card," which may have been left some time before. Your Labrador will not understand why you are shouting, and it won't get your relationship off on a good footing if your pup thinks you are a nasty, hateful tyrant.

Once he has had his vaccinations, get your pup used to relieving himself on a variety of surfaces—grass, sand, gravel, etc. Otherwise, you may end up with a dog that only relieves himself on one surface, which could prove very inconvenient.

Remember always to clean up after your dog, and never leave the house without poop-scoop bags.

To begin with, your puppy will get plenty of exercise just from playing in your yard.

Exercise

Your Labrador pup should have only gentle exercise. Although you may want to enjoy long country walks with the new family member, you will have to wait until his bones and joints have fully formed. Subjecting a pup to strenuous exercise (even for short bouts) can do irreparable damage, affecting him very badly later on. Jumping on and off furniture and racing down the stairs should be prohibited at all times.

In the first few months—until your puppy is four or five months old—exercise should consist of amusing himself in the yard. Obviously, this does not mean that he should be confined to it; you should be introducing him to the outside world as soon as he is protected by his vaccinations (see Chapter Eight). Between six and nine months, your Labrador can enjoy controlled exercise on a lead, building up to short sessions of off-lead exercise. When he is fully grown, he will enjoy as much exercise as you can give him.

If you are in any doubt as to how much exercise your Labrador should be getting, ask your breeder or veterinarian.

EARLY SOCIALIZATION

Like all breeds of dog, your Labrador puppy should be socialized thoroughly. Socialization involves introducing your pup to the world, so that when he grows up he is confident in all situations and with all types of people. It is surprising how many adult dogs get upset by the most innocuous of items, simply because they haven't experienced them before. For example, an early summer pup may spend the first six months of his life without having seen an umbrella or someone wearing a hat. A winter pup may not see someone wearing sunglasses until he is an adolescent. To stop your Lab from developing phobias, introduce him to as much as possible from a young age. A pup is a dry sponge waiting to absorb heaps and heaps of information, so get socializing!

Socialization can still take place while your pup is too young to go out into public places. Ask friends and family to come around and help out with his training. Here's a list of situations you can create at home so that your puppy learns not to be frightened:

- someone carrying an umbrella.
- someone wearing sunglasses.
- someone wearing a motorcycle helmet.
- someone vacuuming.

A well-socialized Labrador will take all new experiences in his stride.

- someone wearing a personal stereo.
- people of both sexes, and all ages and ethnic origins.

You can also put the puppy in the car and drive through a busy area.

When he has had his vaccinations, the period of intensive socialization should really start. Take him to busy shopping centers, join a puppy playgroup at your local training center, show him rollerbladers, skateboarders, and cyclists. Take him on a bus, a train, and the subway. Get him used to different sounds, such as car alarms, fireworks, and the air-brakes used by heavy trucks. The list is endless, but the principle for introducing the pup to each experience is the same:

- Be completely confident. Expose the pup to the experience, and act as if nothing out of the ordinary has happened at all. Labradors are very good at reading people and picking up on any tension. If you are nervous, wondering how your pup will react, he will detect your anxiety and may think there *is* something to be suspicious of.
- If he is a little uncertain of something, ignore it. If you make a big fuss over him, he may think feigned fear is a great way of getting attention, and so exploit this in the future. Instead, carry on as normal.
- If he is really *very* scared, then of course you should remove the cause of his fear (e.g., turn off the vacuum cleaner, or take him away from a skateboarder). You should then distract him with something pleasurable (a game with his favorite toy or a tummy rub).

Never avoid exposing the pup to something he has shown fear of. This will only increase his phobia. If anything, you should make sure the puppy is exposed to it even more.

HEALTHY TREATS

Remember only to use small treats as rewards, or your puppy will soon become overweight. Diced carrot is popular with Labs and is a healthy alternative to other training treats.

You may find it difficult to believe, but some Labradors (and yes, they are in a minority) prefer toy rewards to food ones. This is generally found more in working types than in pet or show Labs.

CLICKER TRAINING

Clicker training involves a small plastic box, which, when pressed with the thumb, makes a "click" sound. When used in conjunction with a treat, it can signal that a reward is coming. Eventually, the sound of the click becomes the reward in itself.

The clicker is a more accurate training tool, as it can be used at the exact moment the dog has done something right. It is a "yes marker," telling the pup he is performing well. Once you have signaled that the dog has earned a reward, you can then give a treat.

Clicker training is particularly useful when training Labs. Because they are so food-obsessed, they can become "silly" in training, over-focusing on the food and not really thinking about what they are doing. You can see Labs in training classes that will go through a whole repertoire of "tricks" in the hope that one of them is what is expected and will earn the reward. For this reason, it is important to train them to an alternative non-food reward, eventually giving treats only at random. This way, your dog will still have to work hard to earn a click, but will not expect—or demand—that a treat is given each time.

For example, if he is wary of the sound of a hairdryer, ask someone to switch it on just for short bursts at a time while you are playing a game with him, and giving him his favorite treat. He is unlikely even to notice the noise. Put the dryer on for longer periods over the course of several troubleshooting sessions.

EARLY LEARNING

No pup is too young to learn. At eight weeks, your pup should start some basic elementary training at home. The younger he is when he starts learning, the easier it will be in the long term.

Recall

Lure-training involves holding a treat and moving it so that the dog follows it. It is an effective way of teaching your pup to come to you—as you know, a Labrador will follow someone with food to the ends of the earth if he thinks he'll be given some of it! The following exercise can be used with very young pups, and gets them used to walking toward you.

- Stand in front of your pup. Hold a treat at the pup's nose level, and encourage him to follow it.

The Labrador is naturally eager to please, and, with the added incentive of food treats, he is an eager pupil.

- Take a step back, still holding the treat out, so that he has to walk forward to you to get to it. Give a click as he walks toward you, and give him the treat and lots of praise when he arrives at you.
- Keep practicing, gradually increasing the distance he has to follow the treat. First one step, then two, then three, and so on. When he has understood the exercise, say "Come."

The next stage involves your remaining stationary.

- With your puppy a short distance away, kneel down, hold the treat out as before and say "Come."
- As he comes, give a click, and reward him with the treat when he reaches you.
- With practice, increase the distance he has to come to you.
- If he is slow coming to you, say his name in an excited way to hurry him along.

Practice the Recall at every opportunity, and as he learns, give the treats on a random basis.

- To fine-tune the exercise, tell the pup to sit in front of you when you recall him.
- Once he will come and sit before you when called, touch his collar with one hand, then give him a treat with the other. This should prevent your dog becoming "collar-shy" when he is older, running off before you can put him on the lead at the end of your walks. Call him over throughout your training sessions, so that he never associates your recall with the end of the walk—rather, with getting a treat (or a click and a treat).

Practice his recall throughout the day—calling him from one room to another, calling him in from the backyard, etc.

Be warned that, as soon as the pup has his vaccinations, he is likely to forget his training altogether. You will have to compete with all the distractions of the big outside world, and will have to be more exciting than all the other dogs and smells he is likely to encounter. Carry the smelliest treats in your pocket (e.g., liver), and give a click whenever he comes when called. In the first few months of him being in a public place, it is worth giving him a treat each time too. When he is reliably coming when called, phase out the treats, so your Lab is always left guessing whether he will get one.

If he won't come when called, run away in the opposite direction. This usually confuses a dog, and he is likely to run after you. Keep running off, and he will learn that he has to keep a very close eye on you!

With a treat held above his head, a puppy will naturally go into the Sit position.

Let your puppy know you have a treat, and then lower it toward the ground.

If, despite your best efforts, your Lab's recall isn't very good, do not let him off the lead in a public place, and seek the advice of a professional dog trainer.

Sit

Lure-training is also one of the easiest ways of teaching a pup to sit.

- Hold a small treat in your hand and show it to the pup, who will try to take the treat.
- Hold it above his head, so that he has to stretch his neck up to reach it, and then put it by the tip of his nose.
- To reach the treat, the pup will have to put his bottom on the floor. As soon as he does, click and give a treat. Then make him feel very clever, with lots of praise and petting.
- With repetition, he will become faster at sitting when you lure him. After 20–50 repetitions he should understand what is expected, and when he is reliably sitting when you hold a treat above him, then introduce the word "Sit."
- Over time, you should phase out the treats, giving them only randomly—for example, when he sits very promptly. This way, you can fine-tune his performance, and encourage him to improve.

TOP TIP

If your pup just doesn't get the hang of what is expected when training the Down exercise, one tip is to sit on the floor with one leg sticking out. Make sure there is enough of a gap between the floor and the leg for the puppy to get underneath. Show the puppy the treat and hold it the other side of your leg, so that he has to crawl under your leg to reach it. Click and treat as soon as he goes down.

When he understands what is expected, say "Down" and he should start lying down without you having to stick out your leg.

Down

Teaching your Labrador to lie down on command is taught in a similar way.

- Put your pup in the Sit position (see page 33). Hold a treat in front of his nose, and then put your hand on the floor, about 8 inches (20 centimeters) in front of him.
- The puppy should follow your hand to try to take the treat. It should be held in your clenched fist, so that the pup will not be able to take it unless you allow him to. Show a little of it, to keep him interested.
- Eventually, he will work out that he has to lie down in order to try to take it out of your hand. The moment his belly hits the floor, give a click, and then give the treat.
- Keep practicing so that, eventually, the pup lies down the moment you hold a treat to the floor, or point to it with your hand. When he reaches this stage, introduce the word "Down."

Wait

It is very easy to teach the Wait command as part of the pup's everyday routine, such as when feeding him.

- Hold the pup's food bowl, and just before you put it down for him, tell him to "Wait."
- Wait for just half a second, then put it down. The meal is his reward for waiting, though it never hurts to praise him too.
- Increase the length of time he has to wait before he is given his bowl.
- If you are using clicker training, then give a click while he sits and waits.
- If he leaps up and down, or tries to climb your leg to get to the food, do not give it to him. Tell him to "Sit," then to "Wait" again, and make him hold on for only a short time. Gradually build up the length of time between the command and giving the meal.

Stay

The Stay exercise is slightly different than the Wait, and requires more patience from the dog. Stays and Waits are always difficult exercises to teach—especially to lively Lab puppies that hate doing nothing. To a pup, Stays are boring, so it's your job to make them fun!

- Put your Labrador in the Sit position. Take one step back, wait a second, click, then return to him. Praise him, give him a treat, and make him feel very special indeed.

Build up the Stay in easy stages.

- If he moves forward when you step back, put him back in position and start again. Only click and treat when he is giving the desired behavior.
- Keep practicing, taking more steps back and making him wait longer before returning to him and giving a treat.
- If he consistently fails at a certain level, return to the previous one. For example, if he won't stay at five steps away for a 15-second wait, practice three steps away for 10 seconds. Only increase the level of difficulty when he has mastered the current stage.
- As before, only introduce the word "Stay" when he fully understands what you require of him.

Lead Walking

If you put a light collar on your Lab pup, he shouldn't be too distracted by it, especially if you play a game with him or have a cuddle shortly after it is put on. Never leave him unsupervised while he is wearing it as it could get caught on something and choke him.

Basic heel work can be introduced from day one of getting your Lab pup home.

- Spend a few minutes several times a day when you encourage the pup to follow you off-lead around the house. Most puppies love following their owners, so you shouldn't have too many problems.
- If the pup shows any reluctance, speak in a higher-pitched, more excited way, or hold a treat or a squeaky toy to encourage him to walk with you.
- Try to encourage him to walk on your left-hand side. When he is walking beside you, give a click.
- After he has followed you for a few steps, stop and give lots of praise and a treat.

When you feel he is ready (i.e., he is walking fairly well off-lead), put a light lead on him and keep it very loose. Provided it is very slack, your Lab pup shouldn't even realize it is on.

- Encourage the pup to walk beside you on your left-hand side, as before.
- The ideal position is where the pup's front legs are level with yours, and where he is walking closely beside you.
- You should encourage him to look at you as he walks. Call his name to get his attention, or hold a treat or a toy in your right hand, which you should hold across your tummy.
- Remember to give a click whenever he is walking well beside you and give a treat at the end.

To begin, encourage your puppy to move confidently on the lead.

- When he knows exactly what is expected (after many practices), say "Heel" so that he learns to associate the word with the action.
- If he pulls too far ahead on the lead, stop, call him back to you and start again. Your pup will soon learn that pulling gets him nowhere fast.

ROUTINE CARE

The Labrador is not a breed that needs a lot of maintenance, but there are still some basic procedures you should get him used to from a young age. It may be fairly easy to wrestle an eight-week-old pup in order to cut his nails, but a fully grown Lab with tickly toes is an entirely different matter. To prevent such difficulties when he is older, get him used to being handled and groomed while he is still an amenable pup.

Spend a few minutes every day touching the pup's feet gently, and inspecting his nails. If he needs his nails cut, use guillotine clippers and shave off just a small amount at a time. Don't cut the quick of the nail. When you inspect his feet, give him a treat so he associates it with a rewarding experience. The more it is done, the more he will get used to it.

A short grooming session will accustom your puppy to being handled.

Do the same when checking inside his ears, and when opening his mouth and inspecting his teeth. It is unlikely that your pup will have dirty ears or teeth at such a young age, but the checks will get him used to being handled when he is older. Get him used to having his teeth brushed gently, too. Use a soft toothbrush or fingerbrush, and special meat-flavored toothpaste (always a favorite with Labs).

You should also get your pup used to having his coat brushed. While you are petting him, brush him gently with a very soft brush initially, and when he is comfortable with it, progress to a harder bristle brush and a metal comb. Make sure you brush down to the skin, rather than simply tickling the surface. Make sure you brush all over—including his armpits, under his tail, etc.

Your Lab should also get used to being handled all over, so lay him on his side, and stroke him gently—including his tummy, under his arms, etc. You will become your veterinarian's favorite client if your Lab accepts being inspected all over without so much as a sigh.

CHAPTER THREE

THE ADOLESCENT LABRADOR RETRIEVER

Many people get a Labrador thinking it is an "easy" breed that will need minimal input. How wrong they are! Yes, the Labrador is versatile and adaptable, and, provided he is well socialized and well trained, he is a joy to live with. However, raising a dog responsibly—whatever the breed—is never easy. It involves a lot of hard work, and this doesn't come to an end when your Lab's puppy days are over. In fact, from about five months to three years of age, your dog may need even more attention. This is the time when your Lab leaves his "oh-so cute" puppyhood and enters the most difficult phase—adolescence.

During his terrible teens, a Labrador has the body of an adult, but he still has the mind and manners of a pup. This can be a pretty lethal combination. It can be compared to taking a five-year-old child off his tricycle and putting him behind the wheel of a Porsche.

Now, when your Lab jumps up to greet you, instead of barely reaching your knee, he can shred your sweater, and send you flying. He has the height to reach all the areas previously barred—particularly kitchen work surfaces with tempting dishes of food. And even though the teething phase is officially over, a Lab can still be very mouthy and destructive, particularly if he is bored and is left on his own.

Many dogs that are given to rescue shelters for rehousing are adolescents. Perhaps the owners become fed up with the chewing, barking, and boisterous behavior when the honeymoon period of puppyhood is over. Perhaps the pup was an impulse buy, and the owners had not bargained on the real commitment involved in looking after and training a fairly large, energetic breed.

To stop your Labrador from becoming another rescue statistic, it is crucial to continue with his training, and to offer firm (but kind) discipline during this difficult time.

Labradors can be boisterous in their dealings with other dogs.

Training Classes

Too many people think their dog's training starts and ends with a ten-week course when the pup is three months old. This is not the case. Puppy training is just an introduction and should not be seen as an education that will last a lifetime.

By the time your pup finishes his first puppy course, he will have learned basic commands, but it is advisable to continue with training throughout the dog's entire adult life. Not only will this improve his all-around obedience, it will also keep your Lab mentally stimulated, it will strengthen your relationship with your dog, and should help to minimize the stress of the terrible teens.

As with choosing a puppy training course, you should visit a class to observe the training methods used before signing up.

It is also worth considering getting involved in one of the many canine sports (see Chapter Five).

As well as being a good release for your Lab's excess energy, sports such as Agility or Flyball help to exercise his mind.

Bullish Behavior

Labradors have a great enthusiasm for life, and, in their dealings with other dogs, this can sometimes translate into boisterous, antisocial behavior. Mixing with dogs of all sizes is an essential part of your Labrador's early education. However, it is equally important that controlled contact with other dogs is continued when your Lab is larger and more rambunctious.

Labradors are generally friendly, sociable dogs, but they need to recognize their own strength. Leaping onto another dog as an invitation to play soon makes enemies in the local park—human as well as canine. Working with your dog in a training class environment will help to teach "park manners," and your Lab will also learn to read the body language of other dogs, and to react appropriately.

The mistake many owners make is to withdraw their dog from training classes when problem behavior starts to become apparent. It is understandable that owners feel embarrassed when their pet starts becoming unruly around other dogs. However, removing the problem dog does not remove the problem behavior, and it will simply re-emerge in another social situation which could have far more serious consequences.

Stick with classes, follow your trainer's advice, and console yourself with the fact that bullish behavior is a phase many dogs go through. If you stop attending classes, it may be a phase your dog never grows out of.

Jumping Up

Your Labrador needs to know his limits at home, too, where his natural exuberance can exceed the boundaries of what is acceptable to you. For example, when you return home after being out for a couple of hours, your loving Lab will be incredibly pleased to see you—acting as if he hasn't seen you for years! This is all very flattering, but it is not so endearing when the force of your Labrador jumping up lands you on the floor.

Of course, a ban on jumping should have been imposed from the word go—although a small puppy is unlikely to knock you over, he needs to understand that jumping up is counterproductive and is not worth doing. However, this is a lesson that is easily forgotten by the ebullient Labrador, and you may well find that your teenager needs a firm reminder that this behavior is unacceptable.

The moment your Lab jumps up, pay him no attention whatsoever. Turn away, fold your arms, and do not even look at him. He should be given attention only when he greets you in a well-mannered way—i.e., not jumping up. Discipline is only as good as the people implementing it, so be sure everyone who comes into contact with your dog knows to react the same way. In no time, your affectionate Labrador will get the message that he only gets attention when all four feet are firmly on the ground.

Jumping up may be endearing in a puppy, but it can become a menace when the dog is fully grown.

The Destructive Labrador

As pups, Labradors are great chewers. Generally, this is outgrown, and the average Lab simply wants to carry things in his mouth (see Chapter Four). There are exceptions, however, and the need to gnaw can be triggered at a moment's notice—particularly if he becomes bored and wants some amusement. Leaving your Labrador at home alone, with nothing to keep him occupied, is asking for trouble.

Labradors are people dogs and hate to be excluded from their family pack. You should never leave your dog at home alone for long periods of time (certainly no longer than three to four hours). If you do need to leave your Lab for a couple of hours, put him in his crate with some tough toys to keep him occupied.

Kongs—hard, rubber toys that have a hollow inside—are enjoyed by most dogs. When you are playing together, the Kong can be thrown, and its unpredictable bounce is a source of great pleasure. What is even more exciting for the food-orientated Labrador is that a Kong can be stuffed with tasty food. Your Lab will have a heck of a time trying to extract the treats—so it is the perfect toy to keep him occupied when he is home alone.

The soft-mouthed Labrador is potentially a great chewer, and this behavior will come to the fore if he is bored or excluded from the family pack.

Remember, a bored dog is a destructive dog, and it is your responsibility to stop this problem from arising. If you fail to give your Lab something suitable to chew, he may well find something of his own, and that is when your relationship with your dog can start to deteriorate.

Separation Anxiety

This is a complex condition where a dog becomes extremely stressed when he is left alone. It should not be confused with destructive behavior that can, understandably, result when a dog is left for long periods at a time. Some over-anxious dogs become upset even if their owner leaves a room for a matter of seconds—some will even try to accompany their owner into the bathroom, becoming very distressed if refused access!

This behavior may be influenced by a number of different factors. Perhaps the dog has had a nerve-wracking experience while left on his own (e.g., a thunderstorm), or perhaps he has developed too close an attachment to his owner and is not confident on his own. Whatever the reason, it is best to consult a behaviorist if there are difficulties, as a professional will be better qualified to deal with the problem.

One way of trying to *prevent* separation anxiety is to get the dog used to spending time apart from you. Even when he is a young pup, your Labrador should get used to sometimes being on his own. A crate (see page 23) is a particularly useful device because you can put your pup in it, and still be visible. Once he is

Separation anxiety stems from a lack of confidence, so the dog is worried about being left on his own.

happy in the crate, you can move it to another room where he can still hear your voice. Eventually, you can move it so you are out of sight and earshot. This should be done for short periods at first, gradually extending to longer sessions as he becomes more confident.

The crate should not be viewed as a prison, where the pup or dog is incarcerated for long periods. It should be your Labrador's "special space," a safe, cozy den where he feels secure. Bedding and safe chew toys will increase the crate's appeal to your pet.

Never make a big fuss of saying goodbye to your Labrador, nor of greeting him when you return, as this will accentuate your absence.

Coming and going is a part of everyday life, and, with sensible handling, your Labrador should be quick to realize that you always come back.

Leave It

This is one of the most common commands you will use during your Labrador's adolescence. "Leave it" can be used when your Lab is about to steal a cookie from the coffee table, or is eyeing up some meat waiting to go into the oven. It can be used as your Lab is about to roll in rabbit droppings (or, worse still, about to eat them), or to stop your oversexed dog from mounting a cushion or your leg. Yes, adolescence is a very trying time for owners!

"Leave it" is one of those commands that is effective because of the way it is said. You should sound stern and authoritative, so your errant Lab knows he won't get away with his bad behavior. As soon as he stops in response to your command, divert his attention immediately. Squeak a toy and throw it for your Lab to fetch, ask him to do a trick for a treat, or ask him to come to you for a cuddle. Good recall skills (see page 31) are essential, as is your "bargaining" power—whatever you have to tempt your dog to you has to be considerably more appealing than what he was doing.

The only fail-safe way of preventing your Lab from stealing is to become neater! This does not only apply to food. Labs love fetching things and giving them as presents to visitors. One owner reported her embarrassment when the postman presented her with a nightgown that

The Labrador is a great opportunist—particularly if food is left within easy reach!

her generous Lab had given as a present in return for the mail!

"Humping" cushions or legs is usually a transitory, adolescent phase, and is easily stopped with a sharp "Leave it" command, followed up by diversionary tactics. The worst thing you can do is to laugh at your dog, or to let him continue doing it. If he thinks that humping is a great way of entertaining his family and of getting their attention, then he may continue to do it even if the hormonal drive has been removed through castration.

NEUTERING

If you do not intend to show or breed from your Labrador Retriever, neutering should be considered. This can have important health benefits.

Male Castration

Castration can prevent testicular cancer and balinitis (inflammation of the glans penis). It also offers a higher degree of protection against prostate disorders in older dogs. If you have a Labrador that displays hypersexed behavior, castration may help to reduce the severity of his symptoms. However, remember that castration will only help this condition if the cause of your dog's bad behavior is the presence of too much testosterone. If bad handling is the cause, castration will not help in the slightest.

If you have a dog that suffers from cryptorchidism (retained testicles), then castration is strongly advised. Labrador breeders are trying to eliminate this hereditary condition. Not only does cryptorchidism disqualify your dog from the show ring, but the condition generates a far higher risk of developing testicular cancer.

If your Labrador is not to be used as a stud dog, many veterinarians now recommend castration. Allowing your dog to act as a stud once and then castrating him has serious side effects for the dog, and encourages hypersexed behavior even after castration.

Bitch Spaying

Neutering also has many advantages for bitches. Spaying eliminates the chance of a bitch developing pyometra (pus-filled womb). When performed prior to the first season, it also greatly decreases the risk of your bitch developing mammary tumors as she gets older. Some veterinarians argue that a complete hysterectomy actually prevents tumors completely.

Some owners believe that spaying causes a bitch to put on weight, but this can be easily avoided through sensible dietary control and plenty of exercise. It has also been suggested that spaying, particularly the spaying of very young bitches, can make females incontinent in later life. The evidence for this is not conclusive, and spaying after the first season may eliminate the problem altogether.

Your vet will advise you as to what is the best age to neuter.

Another consideration to bear in mind is that an unspayed bitch will need to be kept isolated from other dogs for about 21 days twice a year. She may also suffer false pregnancies, which can make some females moody and unpredictable.

The age at which you have your Labrador neutered will depend on your veterinarian. Some recommend that the procedure is carried out at 6–10 months. Others consider it better to neuter earlier (some are even operating as early as 12 weeks).

If you are at all unsure about what is best for your own dog or bitch, talk to your veterinarian, who will help you make the right decision.

CHAPTER FOUR

THE FAMILY DOG

The Labrador is a wonderful family dog. However old he is, a Labrador remains a big kid at heart and loves the company of children who have been taught to respect him. An energetic dog that will relish family walks and outings, the Labrador is also content to curl up by his owner's feet (or on their laps!) at the end of the day and enjoy a good cuddle.

Although the Labrador is renowned for his good temperament, you shouldn't leave anything to chance and assume that your dog and children will automatically become best buddies. It is important to teach them to respect each other—to play with each other gently, and not to play with each other's toys. As with any breed of dog—whatever his size—you must never leave dogs and young children unsupervised.

Once a friendship has been established, they can both enjoy the very special relationship that only dogs and children can share.

A firm foundation of friendship.

CANINE NANNIES

Valerie Higham had grown up with Boxers as family pets. However, when she and her husband decided to start a family, they wanted to find a breed of dog that would be ideal around babies and very young children.

Valerie narrowed down the choice to Golden Retrievers or Labradors, and ultimately decided on Labradors—a decision she has never regretted.

"Our first Labrador was named Sam," says Valerie. "He was a black Labrador, and was about a year old when our daughter, Catherine, was born. Having adopted Sam before we had the children, we thought it was very important to make sure he didn't feel excluded when Catherine arrived. Fortunately, it all worked out well. We lavished attention on Sam and he formed an immediate bond with Catherine.

Copper—in the midst of family life.

"Sam appointed himself as the children's nanny. When Catherine was a baby, we would put her in her crib at night and Sam would stay with her until she fell asleep. Then he would come back downstairs again.

When our other two children were born (Elizabeth came along when Sam was two-and-a-half, and Stephen when Sam was six) he did exactly the same with them."

Valerie was so impressed with Labradors as children's pets that when Sam was getting rather elderly she decided to get another.

"By the time Sam reached the age of eleven, he was partially blind and deaf, and was suffering from arthritis. He was still very good with the children, but you could see it was exhausting him. As our children were still quite young (ten, eight, and five), we decided to get another, younger Labrador. His name was Copper and he was our first yellow Labrador.

"We introduced Copper very slowly and carefully. We were concerned about putting Sam's nose out of joint. We needn't have worried. Sam was absolutely overjoyed to have Copper. It gave him a new lease of life.

"For the children, my Labs have been playmates, confidants, counselors, and teachers. They instinctively know our moods and respond accordingly—life would be so much less without them."

CARING FOR AN ADULT LABRADOR

A Labrador does not need as much time-consuming care as some of the long-coated breeds that require endless grooming. However, keeping on top of your regular doggie chores will save you lots of time in the long run. Spend a few minutes every day brushing the dog and checking him over—this is far better (both for the dog and for you) than a two-hour session once a month. It will also allow you to spot any signs of trouble at the earliest possible stage, which is the key to preventing serious health problems developing.

The low-maintenance Labrador has an easy coat to care for.

Coat

You should bathe your Labrador as little as possible to avoid removing the natural oils that help to clean the coat. The Labrador coat was designed to withstand all weather, and a regular brushing will be far more beneficial than plunging your Lab into a bath. If your dog gets a little muddy, wipe the affected areas with a damp cloth, and dry him thoroughly. Of course, there will be times when your Labrador needs a thorough soak—especially if he has rolled in something disgusting.

Although smaller breeds can be lifted into a bathtub or sink, your back probably won't withstand lifting a 70-odd-lb. (31-kg) Labrador into the bathtub. Even if you are strong enough, your Labrador is likely to panic in the bathtub (even if you use a non-slip mat), and the almighty shake he will give the moment he is out of the bath will soak every inch of your bathroom. Unless you like redecorating, it is probably preferable to bathe your Labrador outside.

Use a very mild shampoo or even plain water. The harsher the shampoo, the more oils will be removed. As a result, the coat will become softer and will pick up dirt more easily. Rinse thoroughly after washing.

Drying

It is very important to dry your Labrador very carefully. He should never go to bed when he is wet, nor lie on a drafty floor. Labradors can get "water tail" if left damp. This is where the tail becomes rheumatic at the base. Often, the tail extends two or three inches from the base, and then the rest limply hangs down.

Teeth

Your Lab should be familiar with having his teeth cleaned from when he was a little pup (see Chapter Two). If meat-flavored toothpaste is used, no self-respecting Lab will refuse the opportunity of satisfying his tummy, and will usually oblige without complaint.

If your Lab is a little jumpy about having a toothbrush poking around his mouth, try gently rubbing his teeth and gums with a fingerbrush (so called because it fits on the end of your finger).

Feeding your Lab food with an abrasive texture will help to remove plaque too. Raw vegetables are particularly useful, and are enjoyed by most Labs (if it's food, they'll eat it!).

Nails

Check your Labrador's nails regularly to see if his nails need trimming. Black and chocolate Labradors seem to have softer nails than yellow Labradors, and they will tend to wear down naturally.

Dewclaws are positioned high up the foot, and, since they will not wear down naturally, they will need regular attention.

If you need to cut the nails (usually if your Lab does not enjoy sufficient road-walking), use guillotine-type clippers, and shave a little of the nail at a time instead of chopping too much off at once. This should prevent you from nicking the "quick" of the nail (the nail's blood and nerve supply) and causing your dog pain. The brown nails of chocolate Labradors and the black nails of black Labs can make it especially difficult to see the "quick," though it is easier with the lighter-colored nails of yellow Labs.

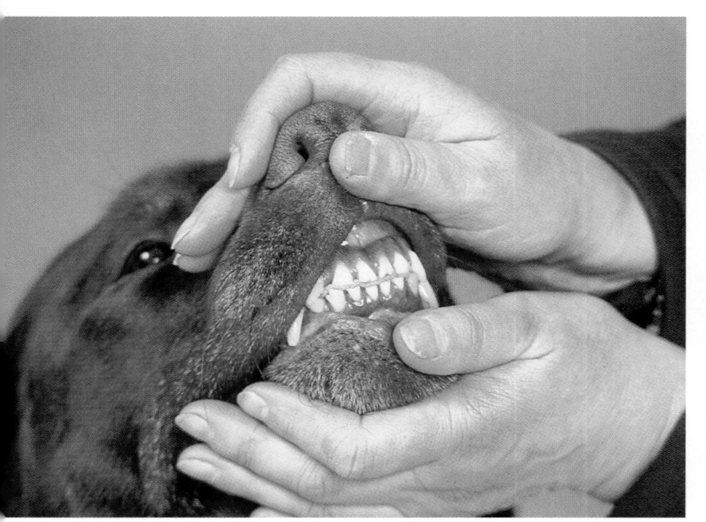

Teeth should be checked regularly. They will need to be cleaned if there is an accumulation of tartar.

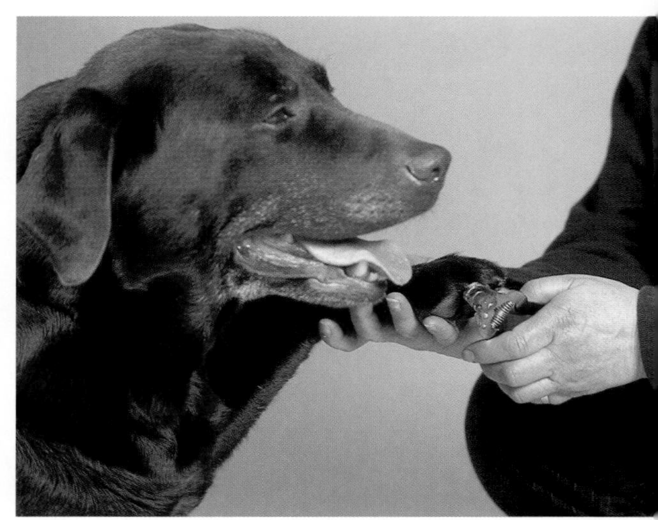

Nails can be trimmed using guillotine-type clippers.

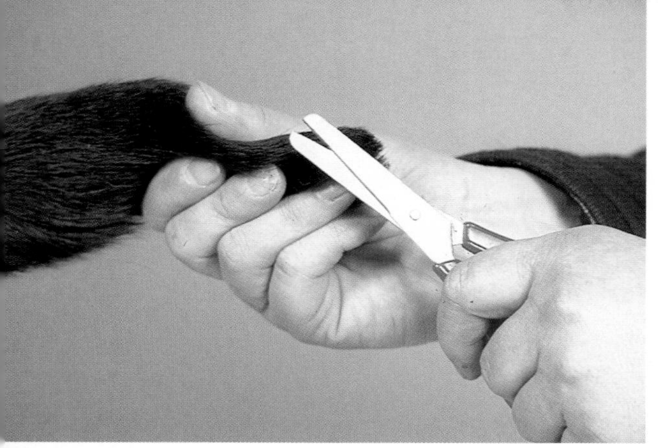

The twizzle—the loose hair at the end of the tail—can be tidied up.

Trimming the Tail

If you show your dog, you will need to trim his tail "twizzle"—the loose hair at the end of the tail. Because the tail narrows to a very fine point, you must be very careful not to cut the tail by accident. Ask a fellow show competitor, or a professional groomer, to show you how best to trim the tail with care.

Other Checks

While you are brushing your dog, spend some time running your hands over him, feeling for any unusual lumps or bumps. Be particularly vigilant for grass seeds. Although they look innocuous, they can cause considerable damage and pain to your Lab. Once embedded in a pad, between the toes, or in an ear, the arrow-type seed works its way further in; the umbrella-like structure grips the skin and prevents the seed from being removed easily.

You should also check your dog's ears for any sign of infection or mites (bad odor, inflammation, pus, wax, scratching ear, shaking head, etc.). If you see any of these signs, you must consult your veterinarian.

Regular ear cleaning is very important in the Lab. Because the Labrador's ears flap forward, air cannot circulate as easily as in the erect-eared breeds, such as the German Shepherd Dog. The damp, warm environment inside the ear may easily become a breeding ground for bacteria or mites if not cleaned regularly.

Diet

A Labrador lives to eat, rather than eats to live. It can be wearing to battle against your dog's insatiable appetite, watching that he is not scavenging or stealing food, and resisting those pleading eyes. However, if you "stick to your guns," and never let your Lab beg for food, you should minimize the problem. The advantage, of course, is that very few Lab owners have to deal with fussy eaters. If your Labrador does go off his food, it is usually a sign that something isn't quite right, so consult a veterinarian.

There are many different types of food on the market. Some people feed canned food, others give fresh meat and vegetables, and a growing number use complete foods (which offer a completely nutritionally balanced meal). Many manufacturers cater to a Labrador's changing needs, with specific formulas for each stage of your dog's life.

Your decision as to which type of food to choose will be influenced by a variety of factors:

- cost considerations.
- convenience (fresh diets can take longer to prepare and are not as easily stored as dry foods).

Food intake must be carefully monitored—the Labrador thinks he is always hungry!

- recommendations from your breeder/friends/ veterinarian.
- health considerations (e.g., your Lab may have a food allergy to a particular ingredient).
- your Labrador's personal taste preferences (though Labs are rarely this discerning and will eat anything with great relish).

As with changing a puppy's diet (page 27), an adult's diet should also be changed gradually to avoid any tummy upsets (though most Labs have the constitution of an ox).

Obesity

The Labrador has a natural disposition to eat, eat, eat, and trying to stop him from getting fat can be a struggle. You will have to learn to lock food away or to keep it in high cupboards where the dog cannot reach. Sacks of dog food should not be kept in a corner of the kitchen, or in a bin where the lid can easily be removed. Your Lab will eat through the bag and then consume most of its contents. Vomiting and diarrhea will follow.

Be very vigilant at Christmas time, and never put edible gifts under the Christmas tree or edible decorations on it. Otherwise, you may come home to find your tree all over the floor, and Aunt Mabel's finest Belgian chocolates in the dog.

Chocolate intended for human consumption can be very toxic to dogs (and can actually kill them if sufficient amounts are ingested). If you suspect your Lab has eaten any chocolate, seek veterinary advice at once. If your Lab has a sweet tooth, only give him chocolate made specifically for dogs.

Exercise

Labradors are very energetic dogs, and once they are fully grown at about a year old, they can enjoy more strenuous exercise. As a rough guide, your Lab will need around 20–30 minutes of exercise twice a day. Some need more, some need less, so adjust to your individual dog.

It is not necessarily the quantity, but rather the quality, that counts. A 25-minute aimless plod around a flat, boring park, is not nearly as beneficial as a 15-minute walk through woods, chasing squirrels and investigating rabbit scents. As well as receiving sufficient physical exercise, the Lab's brain needs to be stimulated too. Most will relish retrieving balls on their walks—especially from water—and this exercises both body and brain.

Fetch!

The Labrador instinct to retrieve is built-in, and rarely needs extensive teaching. The following exercise helps to stir their natural instinct, and can be done with adults and puppies alike.

CHOCOLATE LABRADOR

"At the end of a recent weekend spent entertaining my family, I shut Samurai, my two-year-old Lab, in the house while I bid adieu to my visitors. When I returned, Sami had an empty bread basket in his mouth. Upon closer scrutiny of the house, I noticed pieces of a candy dish, though no sign of the foil-wrapped chocolates it contained. As I did not know how many candies he had eaten, I called the vet.

"The vet did not think that the amount of chocolate he consumed would be harmful considering his size, but I was told to watch him in case he became lethargic (I began to think perhaps I should give him a bit of chocolate every day in the hope he *would* become a little lethargic!). The vet did say that I should give Samurai some bread. I responded that the dog had self-medicated, as he followed the candies with some rolls left in the basket on the table. What a smart dog!"

Pamela Spindola, Santa Ana, California

Samurai: A quick recovery after a lightning binge.

- Find a soft dog toy (preferably one that is squeaky) that is the right size and shape to be carried in your dog's mouth.
- Sit your dog down, squeak the toy to get his attention, and put the toy a little distance from him.
- Tell him to "Get it" and he will go over and investigate. The moment he puts the toy in his mouth, encourage him excitedly to you, so he brings the toy with him.
- If he doesn't take the toy in his mouth, pick the toy up and shake it gently in front of his face to encourage him to play with it in his mouth. Make a big fuss when he does.

Keep practicing, with the toy being put at a greater distance from your dog. Eventually, you will be able to get to the stage of throwing it some distance in long grass, so your Lab has to do some elementary searching for it (page 76). Labradors love playing games, and retrieving toys will really liven up your exercise periods together.

Taking a Dip

Labradors love to swim, and this instinctive need obviously dates back to when they assisted fishermen in Canada. If they see water, however deep, they will want to dive in. The Labrador is one of the few breeds that can swim in an inch of water. Show him a puddle, and he'll somehow manage to submerge himself in it fully!

Be very careful where you allow your Lab to go for a dip. Never let him jump in water where

EXERCISING YOUR LABRADOR

The Labrador was bred to work, and he should be kept fit and healthy with regular exercise.

SAFE TOYS

Just as you should check toys that you give children, so you should investigate your Labrador's toys. Check that balls and other toys are the correct size, and won't get stuck down your dog's throat. Squeaky toys should be checked regularly, as the plastic squeakers can work loose and can be swallowed. Any toys that show damage or wear should be discarded.

If your dog is a real chewer, only give him really tough toys. Not only will this save you money in replacing damaged toys, but it will also prevent him from chewing and possibly swallowing parts of toys he has chewed to pieces.

Never throw sticks for your dog. Although it seems harmless enough, many dogs have been seriously injured by them.

you can't see what is underneath, and make sure there are no strong currents that could endanger your dog.

Try to establish some control over your Lab when you are near water. He should only go in when you give the command, and he should respond promptly to the Recall when he is in the water.

RESCUE DOGS

If one breed, more than any other, has a rescue problem, it is the Labrador. Sadly, it is the breed's immense popularity that has also proved its downfall, and there are all too many Labs in rescue shelters, waiting to be found homes.

The fact that the Labrador is so well loved, and appeals to so many people, means that the breed is often used in advertising. People see charming little pups on television without fully realizing that they grow into 70–80-lb. boisterous dogs, who are forever clearing the coffee table with one swipe of their strong, animated tails.

VETERAN CARE

If your Labrador has been healthy and active during his youth, the chances are that he will continue to enjoy good health throughout his old age. On average, a healthy Labrador can be expected to live between 12 and 14 years, with some bloodlines living for up to 15 or 16 years.

All too often, a Labrador needs rehousing through no fault of his own.

THIRD TIME LUCKY

Carole Baker is a volunteer helper for the Labrador Rescue Trust. Part of Carole's job is to assess dogs for rehousing and help find them suitable new homes. Carole is very dedicated to caring for Labs that fall on hard times, and likes to take her work home with her!

"I had a call from a lady who had to part with her 11-year-old Labrador, Barnaby," explains Carole. "The owner's husband had left her, she had several children and could not afford the expensive veterinary treatment Barnaby needed for a skin condition he had.

"I went to collect him, only to find a complete wreck. He had no coat from behind his shoulder blades, all along his back, to his tail. He was bare, sore, and probably 30 percent underweight. I took one appalled look at him and whisked him straight to my veterinarian.

"Once there, we discovered that, on top of his bad skin and weight problem, his lymph glands were up and he had damage to one eye. As we were talking, we found we were standing in an ever-widening puddle—then we realized he was incontinent too!

"Barnaby was in such a terrible state and was with people he didn't know, but he still stood there—in a puddle of urine—and gave a little wag. That really breaks your heart. After going through so much, and being in considerable discomfort, he was still prepared to believe that people were on his side—even though he had never seen any evidence of this.

"Barnaby was prescribed antibiotics, and a medicated bath three to four times a week. When we left, the vet said he didn't know if Barnaby would last days, weeks, or months.

"By then I had already made up my mind that, given Barnaby's age and everything that was wrong with him, I wouldn't be able to rehouse him and that he would be coming home with me. I made him an impromptu bed of towels and bedding in the kitchen, near my other two Labs, and the next day I bought him his own bed. He loved it. I don't think he had ever had his own bed before. He wouldn't get out of it! He had to be gently tipped out! He slept and slept and slept, and ate and ate and ate.

"My dogs are used to having waifs and strays passing through. They usually look up and sigh as if to say 'Here's another one.' But they were different with Barnaby. Usually, they will sniff a new dog and they will all go off and play together, but they were very gentle with him. They must have seen and smelled that he was ill.

Barnaby—happy and settled in his new home.

"A year passed, and Barnaby has made a full recovery, though his immune system is shot to pieces. As soon as he is ill, the weight just falls off him. A few months ago, he had an infected hematoma on his ear and not only did he lose weight, but the incontinence returned too. He just has no resistance.

"Barnaby has settled well and now sleeps on the sofa with my other male dog. He is a real gentleman, but occasionally enjoys a mad five minutes when he lets his hair down and races around with my other dogs. He is affectionate and a terrific character. He is simply fabulous and I love him to pieces."

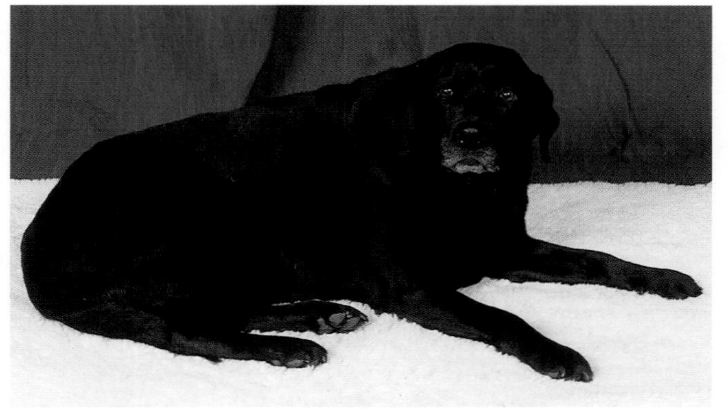
The older dog deserves special consideration.

A dog is considered a veteran at the age of seven, though some dogs may show no signs of aging at this time—it very much depends on the individual dog. At whatever age your Lab starts showing the first signs of aging, you should be aware of how your care for him may need to be adapted.

As well as developing a few white hairs around the muzzle, your Lab may slow down a little. He may need less exercise, and hence less food (or food specifically designed for the older dog) so he doesn't fall victim to obesity. His nails may need to be trimmed more frequently because they are not being worn down as quickly.

Many Labradors may become a little more stiff as a result of aging bones, joints, and muscles. Cold floors, or sleeping in a draft can exacerbate such conditions, so make sure your dog has somewhere warm to rest. If your dog has a history of hip dysplasia (HD) (see Chapter Eight) then he is quite likely to develop arthritis in his hip joints. A healthy diet, regular exercise, and appropriate treatment from your veterinarian is essential to help minimize the effects.

All older Labradors need more sleep and should be allowed to rest undisturbed, so supervise playful pups or children who may have other ideas!

Even if there appears to be nothing wrong with your dog, you should still bring him to the veterinarian every six months or so. If caught early enough, many conditions that could seriously threaten your dog's health if left untreated can be cured or managed.

Character Changes

Your dog's character may undergo some change too. Some oldies become a little more solitary, others become more "clingy" and crave more cuddles. Some can take a strong dislike to change. For example, if you move a dog's bed from one room to another, he may behave in a depressed or mildly aggressive fashion.

Although renowned for their affectionate natures, Labradors can be stubborn. As they age, some dogs may become gradually more obstinate. By far the most common display of this is "voluntary deafness." This is where your Labrador may appear to be going a little deaf when you ask him to sit, or to go to his bed, but makes a remarkable recovery whenever you are opening a can of food!

Possibly the most important factor in ensuring your Labrador reaches a grand old age is to provide him with plenty to keep his interest in life alive.

MURPHY'S LEGACY

Anne Taylor is a top breeder, exhibitor, and judge from England. She has been through the grieving process many times throughout years of experience with the breed, and says it never gets any easier. One dog in particular, Murphy, affected her especially badly.

"I bred Murphy myself," says Anne. "His parents were a Show Champion and a Champion. I had always kept bitches before and wasn't intending to keep Murphy at first. I had chosen to keep a bitch for the show ring, and intended to sell Murphy to a private home after I had kept him a couple of months just to keep the bitch puppy company. Another breeder saw Murphy and commented on what potential he had, and I realized that, in fact, he was the most promising of the two, so I kept him.

"He went to his first show when he was six months, and from then on kept winning and winning. He even became the breed record-holder.

"Murphy was a special dog—not just because he did a lot of winning. He went everywhere with me, and he was my best friend.

"Losing Murphy has been the most painful ordeal for me. He was a perfectly healthy dog and then one morning, when he was 11, he was sick. Labs being Labs, I thought he had eaten something he shouldn't have, but he continued to be ill. He was jaundiced and refused to eat—very unusual for Labradors.

"I took him to the vet who thought it could be a virus, and Murphy was put on an IV. Neither myself nor the veterinarian thought it was anything too serious. He became dehydrated. I still wasn't at the point where I thought 'Enough is enough,' as I believed he'd just shake off the suspected virus and be as right as rain in a day or two. This went on for about a month, with him deteriorating slowly.

"In the end the vet decided we should open him up, and he found a huge tumor. I gave the vet permission to let Murphy go under the anaesthetic.

"I was devastated. I'm lucky to always have a dog or two around to help me with the grieving process—I feel very sorry for people who have one dog, and then come back from the vet to an

Murphy in the driver's seat, taking care of his nephew.

empty house. I always advise people—if they can—to have a second dog, about four or five years younger than their first. Then they will never have to face suddenly being without a dog. I often get calls from people who desperately want a puppy because they have just come back from the vet, having lost their other Labrador. Some people call after losing their dog six months before—at first they thought they could live without a dog, but in reality, just couldn't do without.

"Although I find having other dogs around helps me, I don't think people should believe they can replace their pet. All dogs are individuals. Some people get the same breed and color of dog, and even call it the same name. I know some people who are on their third Sooty.

"Different people deal with grief in different ways. Non-dog-loving friends who say 'What's the fuss about? It was only a dog' don't help! In some ways, losing a dog is like losing a child. You have lived with this dog for many years and have become very attached. Yes, he was a dog, but what's the point of having an animal that you do not love? And if you love a pet, you will grieve when it is no longer there.

"Losing a pet is part and parcel of owning one. After the initial pain, you start to remember the good times. I cry when I go through photos of Murphy still, but I also remember all the happy times we shared. Plus, being such a successful show dog, Murphy was used extensively at stud, so has lots of children and grandchildren and great-great grandchildren. I can see bits of him in his descendants, and it is comforting to know he will always live on, giving as much joy to their owners as he did to me."

Do remember that all Labradors are individual—some may march forth into old age with the youth and vitality of a pup. Only you will know exactly what your Labrador needs—and this knowledge and understanding will come from many years of sharing your life with him. Remember that any changes in behavior usually have a reason. Knowing your dog well should mean that you are able to see the symptoms of illness in your Labrador before it becomes too serious. A quick visit to the veterinarian hopefully should be all that is required to put things right.

Saying Goodbye

Arthritis, cancer, and heart-related problems are the major killers of Labradors. Some dogs get slower and slower, and eventually it becomes too painful for them to move; some develop cancer and their condition may progressively deteriorate. Others may die in their sleep. If we could decide how our pets were to end their lives, most of us would wish them to die peacefully this way. In reality, it is not always this simple, and difficult decisions have to be made about when to intervene and end any suffering.

Deciding to put a well-loved pet to sleep is never easy; the most important thing to consider is your dog's well-being—his feelings come before your own. You might be heartbroken at the prospect of losing your Labrador, but if he is in pain and the veterinarian can do no more, your dog's well-being should be your sole consideration. Your dog cannot verbally tell you he has had enough, but after living with your Labrador, you will know when it is time to say goodbye.

CHAPTER FIVE

BROADENING HORIZONS

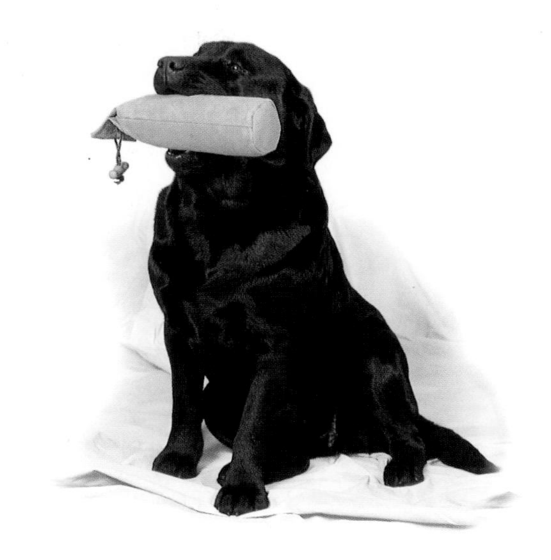

Labradors are not lazy dogs. Yes, they can enjoy a good snooze at their owners' feet in the evening, but they would not be satisfied if their daily routine was always this inactive. However many generations they are removed from the first Newfoundland/St. John's dogs of Canada, the working spirit still courses through their veins, and it is cruel not to give your hard-working Lab the physical and mental activity he enjoys and excels at.

There are canine sports to suit most people—from fast, furious Flyball to the more leisurely track. Read on to find a hobby you can both enjoy together.

Canine Good Citizen

The American Kennel Club and Kennel Club of England have introduced programs to raise awareness of responsible dog ownership and to try to instill good manners in their nations' canines.

The "Good Citizen" programs test various aspects of a dog's behavior, assessing how well the dog is socialized (e.g., whether he will accept being approached and petted by a stranger), and his basic obedience (e.g., whether he can walk well on the lead, and respond to basic commands). As the AKC program explains, the dog should be

- one that the judge would like to own;
- one that would be safe with children;
- one they would welcome as a neighbor;
- one that makes his owner happy while not making someone else unhappy.

The KC has three levels of difficulty (bronze, silver, and gold), and the AKC has just one test. For full details of what is required for your country's Good Citizen program, contact your national kennel club.

The Working Gundog

Whether you agree with shooting or not, there is no denying your Labrador's gundog heritage.

A lot of hard work goes into training a Labrador for Field Trials.

Once imported from Canada, the breed was developed as a retriever of shot game, so it is no surprise that the urge to retrieve is very strong in the breed.

Some Labs are content just retrieving balls on their walks, but some need more of a stimulating challenge—and gundog work offers exactly that.

Role of the Retriever

A retriever should accompany his handler on a shooting situation, and retrieve only when instructed to do so. The dog can be guided by his handler (by hand signals and whistle commands), but the dog should never become a "remote controlled dog"; he should always be able to work independently. He should be able to retrieve in a variety of situations, taking to water if necessary. The dog should be soft-mouthed, ensuring the item retrieved is not damaged in any way.

If you are interested in gundog training, join a specialist gundog club. You must make sure your Lab has a thorough grounding in basic obedience training, however, before embarking on a more challenging course.

Working (Retriever) Tests

Tests came about as a means for the shooting people to train their dogs out of season (i.e., in the summer). Over time, the training classes evolved into competitive events.

Tests simulate a day's shoot, so are a good start if you want to graduate on to the actual shooting conditions of Field Trials. However, if you do not approve of shooting live game, you can stick with Tests, and train only with a canvas dummy. As long as your Labrador is retrieving, he'll be happy!

Tests assess your dog's ability to retrieve, handle (degree of obedience to handler's commands), mark (find fallen game/dummy), and be steady (stay until told to do otherwise)—all essential qualities in a gundog.

FINDING A CLUB

Contact your breed club, or national kennel club for details of your nearest gundog training club.

Sound Confidence

Just because the breed was developed to be a gundog does not mean that all Labradors are instantly comfortable with gunfire. Once a dog becomes gun-shy, it can be very difficult (sometimes impossible) to rid him of his phobia, so careful, gentle introduction is crucial.

Hopefully, the breeder would have started socializing your puppy to startling noises from a young age, dropping stainless steel bowls on kitchen floors, etc., while your pup is feeding from his dam, being petted, or playing a fun game. When you bring your pup home, you should continue to associate loud noises with enjoyable experiences.

A gundog's first experience of gunfire is usually of a starting pistol or dummy launcher. At first, the sound should be at a considerable distance from your dog, ensuring the volume is at a minimum.

As soon as the pistol or launcher has been fired, reward your Lab with a treat. Although a game with a toy is a far more enjoyable treat for some Labs (difficult as it may be to believe), do not reward your dog with a game of retrieve upon hearing gunshot. If your Lab learns to retrieve on the signal of gunfire, he is likely to become unsteady, racing off before being given permission to do so.

Only when he is comfortable with this sound should you progress to moving the sound closer to him. Always move the gun or launcher closer to your dog only in small increments, and move the sound away again if your dog is at all alarmed or nervous of the noise. Never rush, and always ensure progress is slow but steady. As with all forms of training, keep sessions short.

The Retrieve comes instinctively to a Labrador, but it is important to introduce control and discipline.

Training Retrieve

Right from a very young age, Labradors show their willingness to retrieve. You should encourage this instinct whenever possible. Remember never to shout at your dog for picking up and carrying something—even if it is inconvenient or inappropriate. For example, if your Lab is carrying your slippers around, rendering them a soggy mess, you should not shout at him. To do so would discourage him from carrying something in the future. Instead, praise and reward him (though never with a treat—see below). Then take the item, and give him something appropriate to carry and retrieve instead—such as a dummy.

Only give your Lab soft things to retrieve, such as a knotted sock, or a canvas dummy. Giving him hard items, such as wooden/plastic dumb-bells, may encourage him to develop a hard mouth. If you are interested in gundog work with game, you can get your Lab used to holding a variety of textures by fixing rabbit skin to a dummy or putting a feathered wing in a stocking.

- Throw a soft item for your Lab pup or dog (such as a knotted sock). He will instinctively run up to it, and will probably pick it up in his mouth.
- The moment he does so, call him to you in an excited way, and praise him when he brings his "retrieve" to you.
- Teach him to sit when he comes (see page 33), and take the sock from him.
- Then praise and pet him, and reward him by having another game of retrieve!

Note, it is preferable not to give your Lab a food treat when he brings a retrieve to you, as it could encourage him to drop the dummy or game in anticipation of the treat.

RUNNING ERRANDS

In your garden, your Labrador is likely to perform outstanding retrieves, bringing to hand every time. In other situations (such as in Test or Trial situations), however, some dogs can forget all their training. With so many interesting sights and smells in such a wide open area, there are too many temptations for the ill-prepared Lab.

Train your dog in a variety of situations. If he keeps insisting on running away from you, put him on an extending lead, and slowly haul him in to you. Your errant Lab will soon realise there is no point in running away. Most Labs are only too keen to bring the retrieve to you, however – because it usually means another will be thrown for them.

Taking Direction

Your Labrador should learn to follow your directional signals—left, right, and back. Some gundog trainers use one command for left or right (such as "Get on"), distinguishing the direction with a hand signal. The command to get the dog to retrieve from behind him is "Back."

- Put your dog in a Sit-Stay about 20 yards in front of you, and throw a dummy to fall behind him.
- He will probably half-turn to see where it is. Tell him "Back" and put your hand up. His

interest in what is behind him would have been aroused the moment the dummy was thrown, so he won't need much encouraging to investigate.

- With practice, he will soon understand what "Back" and the hand signal mean.

When you think your Labrador has fully understood, you can test his ability further.

- Put your Lab in a Sit-Stay.
- Ask a friend to put a dummy behind the dog, and ensure your Lab sees neither the friend nor the dummy.
- Then tell your Lab to go "Back" and put your hand up. Hopefully, even though he hasn't seen the dummy being thrown, the verbal command and hand signal will still send him in the right direction. His faith in you will be rewarded when he finds the dummy!

Stop!

You should be able to stop your Lab in his tracks wherever he is and whatever he is doing. This can be very difficult—particularly when your Lab is having such a good time retrieving. Training your dog to stop is actually relatively simple, however, but it is crucial that it is done slowly and steadily.

- Walk your Lab on a lead (see page 35). After a while, stop, and blow one long note through your Stop Whistle. (Your training club will tell you how to get hold of such equipment.)
- Ask your Lab to "Sit."
- Pause, then walk on.
- Practice regularly, so that your Lab learns to associate the whistle command with the action (stopping).
- When he is well-practiced (and not before), remove the lead, and repeat as before.
- When he always stops and sits when the whistle is blown, you should progress to the next level. This is where you blow the whistle to stop your dog, but you continue walking on. When your Lab stops, you know you have mastered it! Such cleverness deserves extra-special praise.

Hand signals are used to indicate directions.

WORK AND PLAY

Liz and John Barnes have always had dogs. When they moved to a rural area, John took up shooting, and the couple had the opportunity of seeing gundogs at work.

"When John started shooting, we needed a dog to pick up the game," says Liz, from Elstead, England. We bought our first purebred Lab, Emma, when she was six months old—and ruined her! She was well bred from working lines, but John and I were still quite ignorant and didn't always know what we were doing.

"We bred from Emma and kept two pups—Blondie and Daisy. Because we had moved somewhere close to a river, we needed our dogs to retrieve in water and across to another bank, where shot game could sometimes fall.

"Blondie and Daisy were fine crossing the water to the bank, but then wouldn't come back! They'd just stay there, hunting! Someone suggested we contact a trainer, and we joined a gundog club. I was amazed to learn what you could actually get these dogs to do!

"We entered Working Tests, which we enjoyed a lot and decided to give Trials a go.

"After my first Trial, I swore I would never do it again. It was like going to the dentist but 1,000 times worse! Daisy didn't actually do anything wrong—but the pressure and nerves were overwhelming. It was addictive, though. Within a couple of weeks, I had calmed down, and couldn't stop myself finding out about the next Trial!

"From then on, we got more and more involved, and bred more dogs. Trials are our life now. John is chairperson of one gundog club, and I'm chairperson of another.

"You develop a very close bond when working with your dog. Some people say you can train a Lab while feeding the chickens, but you must still put a lot of work into training. If you haven't been thorough, it will come out in the end.

"One of the high points of our gundog careers was when John made Jim up to a Field Trial Champion in just three days. Another was in 1997 when one of our boys—Teddy—won the Dog Field Trial class at Crufts Dog Show. When you win a Trial or get placed, you are issued with a studbook number which allows you to enter the Field Trials class at Crufts every year. The class is assessed by a show judge. We didn't handle Teddy that day—it was done by a friend, who is experienced in the craft of showing a dog to his best ability. It was nerve-wracking watching him in the ring, but it was great when he won. It's always a good compliment when someone tells you that you have a nice-looking dog—as well as an intelligent one."

John Barnes with (left to right) Blondie, Daisy, and Emma.

AGILITY

Agility is a fast-growing sport throughout the world. It began in the U.K. in the late 70s as entertainment at the Crufts show and is based on equestrian jumpers' events. The dogs, who are off-leash, are guided by the handler through a series of obstacles that includes long and high jumps, tunnels, tires, weave poles, a pause table, A-frame, seesaw, and an elevated plank called a dog walk. The dog and handler team must negotiate the obstacles in the proper order and within a set time.

Once your dog has mastered some basic obedience—Sit, Down, Stay, Come—you are ready to start Agility. Since the obstacles must be taught carefully and safely, it is best to enroll in a class. Agility is so popular that there are many Agility training clubs. Ask your Kennel Club for details. If you are interested in finding out more about Agility, visit a show, where you will be able to watch the dogs, and talk to some handlers. There are also some very informative books and videos available.

The Agility competitor must jump confidently over hurdles.

Over

The competitor is expected to jump over various hurdles and across a long (broad) jump.

The hurdles have easily displaceable bars that fall if the dog bumps into them. This protects the competitors from injuring themselves, but also means complete accuracy is required—the slightest knock, and the bar falls and the clumsy competitor incurs a penalty.

The long (broad) jump is made up of several sections that are put together to make the desired length of jump. Start with just one section, so your Labrador can build up gently. Never overdo it before he is ready—not only could he injure himself, but his confidence could suffer too. A restrain recall (where someone holds the dog, while you stand the other side of the jump and call him to you) is a successful training method for this piece of equipment and the hurdles.

EASY DOES IT

As with all types of exercise, a Labrador should not be expected to do any form of strenuous exercise until he is a year old, when his bones and joints are strong enough to cope.

Weaving demands speed and accuracy.

Through

The dog should weave through upright poles, race through tunnels (both the collapsible, cloth tunnel and the rigid open tunnel), and leap through a tire that is raised off the ground.

Your Agility training club will explain how to teach these obstacles, but to give you an idea, here's an exercise you can try at home.

- Place some bamboo garden canes in a straight line in your yard. Make sure they are quite tall canes, as you do not want your dog accidentally poking his eye on one of them.
- Move the first cane to the left, the second to the right, the third to the left, etc., until you end up with two parallel lines, with enough room between them for you to walk through with your Labrador.
- Walk your dog down the middle of the two lines, say "Weave" and praise and treat him when you get to the end.
- Move the poles in an inch, and repeat.
- As the poles are moved closer to each other, your dog will no longer be able to walk straight through, and will have to maneuver through them, moving slightly to the left and the right.
- It helps if you hold a toy or a treat in front of his nose and guide him through the poles with your hand.
- Remember always to praise and reward him at the end of the obstacle.
- With time and practice, he should be able to speed up, and get into a fast but comfortable rhythm where he "bounces" through the poles.

Making Contact

The A-frame (a ramp in the shape of an "A"), seesaw, and dog walk (plank raised off the ground with a ramp at the start and end) have a contrasting color painted on the ends of the ascending and descending sides. This area is called the contact zone or contact point and the

The contact points on the A-frame are as the dog climbs on, and as he climbs off.

dog must touch these areas when tackling each obstacle.

The principle for teaching each of these pieces is the same. To give you an idea of how to teach contact obstacles, here's an exercise for the dog walk.

- Put your Lab on a lead, and walk him up on to the first contact point.
- When his paws are on the marked areas, stop, give him a treat, and praise him.
- Walk slowly and steadily on to the level section of the walk, praising and reassuring your Lab the whole time.
- Walk down the other side and, when your Lab touches the contact point at the end, repeat as before—pausing, praising, and giving a treat before leaving the obstacle.
- Practice will quicken the pace, but it is important to make sure your Lab always knows to slow a little when getting on and off the walk, or else he may injure himself (and incur a penalty). It isn't usually a problem with Labs, though, as they love lingering on the contacts, hoping for another treat!

Pause

The dog is also expected to jump on to a table, and lie down until he is instructed to move on to the rest of the course. This involves the Jump command (see page 65), and the Down and Stay commands (see Chapter Two).

OBEDIENCE

Once your Lab has mastered basic puppy Obedience (Chapter Two), you might like to consider Competitive Obedience. Watching an experienced dog and handler performing Obedience is quite magical—they work as a close team and the level of expertise can be daunting if you are an absolute beginner. But everyone has to start somewhere, so take every step slowly, and gradually you will both progress to the more difficult exercises and levels.

There are two basic exercises for Obedience that are in every test in some form—the recall and heeling. Sabine Platten, as featured in the case history on page 70, gives the following advice for tackling these two essential Obedience exercises. Even if you don't take up Obedience, they are still useful for fine-tuning your dog's basic recall and heelwork as learned in Chapter Two.

The most important thing to remember is that Obedience should be fun for you both, and should improve your relationship with your dog. As Sabine says: "Labradors are quite willing to work with you; they simply have to

TRANSATLANTIC DIFFERENCES

There are some differences between how Obedience is performed in the US and how it is performed in the UK.

In the US, Obedience contains aspects of UK Working Trials (e.g. long and high jumps). This may explain why the Companion Dog and Utility Dog titles in US Obedience are used in UK Working Trials.

BALOO BLUES

Roberta Earle has been involved in Agility for three years, during which time she has seen the most extraordinary changes in her black Lab, Baloo.

"Winning a blue first-place ribbon in Agility was beautiful, but the changes in Baloo were truly remarkable," explains Roberta, who is from Strafford, Pennsylvania. "Agility helped restore Baloo's faith in the world.

"When Baloo arrived at my house, she was an unhappy, frightened 18-month-old Labrador Retriever. She had no confidence in herself or the people around her, and unfamiliar people or situations frightened her.

"Baloo's first family had several small children and they wanted a happy, friendly family pet. However, Baloo is the type of dog who needs a structured life and a 'job', and she did not respond well to a busy household. The family returned her to the breeder, who was committed to finding the right home for Baloo. Since I do Obedience and Agility, my household was perfect for her. Less than a year later, she was happily and confidently running through tunnels and leaping over jumps.

"I discovered Agility while attending a training seminar. The seminar focused mainly on Obedience and solving behavior problems. However, the instructor demonstrated some techniques for training dogs using Agility obstacles. Agility looked like fun!

"Agility training combines two activities that are favorites with Labradors—eating and playing. With food and praise as a reward, they quickly learn to negotiate the obstacles.

"Both of my Labradors thoroughly enjoy Agility. However, each dog has his or her own unique style. Maggie likes speed and does not worry about accuracy. She quickly learns new behaviors and loves to race around demonstrating her skills. As a result, she frequently knocks over jump bars. Baloo's approach is the opposite. She has a strong desire to be correct. All obstacles are performed very carefully and very accurately. She rarely makes a mistake.

"From the first class to the present day, Maggie's enthusiasm for Agility has not diminished. For her, it is the closest thing to heaven on earth—she receives treats and praise for doing the things that she likes to do!

"Baloo was slower to embrace Agility. At first, she was unsure. She saw Maggie run through the tunnel but she had no desire to approach that scary thing! After about three weeks of daily training (and lots of treats and patience), Baloo finally ran through a six-foot-long tunnel. She was smiling and so excited! She looked as though she had conquered the world. Each obstacle became easier and easier for her. She now competes successfully at an advanced level.

"Both of my dogs and I derive tremendous pleasure from working as a team. Agility is a wonderful sport that you and your Labrador can enjoy together."

Baloo's success in Agility helped to build her confidence.

be shown what to do. To quote my first Obedience instructor, 'teach your puppy with love in your voice and love in your hands'."

Recall

Teach the Recall the moment you bring your puppy home. Keep wonderful treats in your pocket and reward the pup whenever he comes to you when called. Call him often, taking advantage of a very young pup's desire to be with you. Hug, pet, and treat the pup when he comes, then send him back off to play.

Never associate the word "Come" with anything that your Lab would perceive as negative, such as clipping toenails, cleaning ears, or anything else he could deem unpleasant.

- Once your Labrador understands "Come" and reacts quickly, ask a friend to restrain him as you move a short distance away, then call him to you.
- Increase the distance and, as your Lab succeeds, gradually add distractions, such as arranging for another dog or person to walk past.
- Teach your dog that "Come" always means good stuff, and he will blast his way to your side.

Work on the Recall, making sure it is always a positive experience.

Keep your Labrador focused during Heelwork.

Heeling

Heeling is a life skill for your Lab. The first step is to teach your dog to pay attention to you while walking (he must be taught that it is possible to look somewhere other than where he is going).

- Start with your Labrador sitting in front of you, treats in your left hand.
- Begin to walk backwards, rewarding every few steps while the dog follows.

A TRAINED DOG IS A HAPPY DOG

Sabine Platten from Malvern, Pennsylvania, firmly believes that Obedience can improve your relationship with your dog—and can be fun for you both too.

"I am forever grateful to the breeder of my first pet Labrador, Alix. She strongly recommended puppy kindergarten training and Obedience classes. I took her advice and enrolled. We did our homework and—presto!—we were hooked. Alix, a yellow Lab, seemed to love it as much as I did. Our instructor thought we had potential for competition, so we set our sights on a Companion Dog title.

"Obedience tests consist of individual exercises (e.g., heeling with changes of pace and direction, both on-leash and free; recalls; retrieves; scent discrimination), and group exercises (e.g., long sit-stay and down-stay). Labradors are wonderfully suited to Obedience work, as they are to most things—hence their popularity. They learn how to think quickly and they are biddable, happy workers.

"Our competitive career had its humorous moments since Alix has a wonderful imagination. At one trial, on the final exercise (coming when called) she covered half the distance between us and decided that the jumping in the adjoining ring looked more fun. She veered off, jumped the ring fence, and then jumped the high jump, much to the surprise of the Golden Retriever coming over the same fence from the opposite direction!

"On another occasion, during the stationary exercises (e.g., sit-stay, down-stay), while she maintained her down position, she ate every dandelion in front of her and cleared a semicircle covering about one-and-a-half feet. Did I mention that Obedience requires a very good sense of humor?

"On the day we received our Companion Dog title, Alix did herself proud. During the three-minute down-stay, the dog next to her began to sniff her face and under her ears and poked her with his paws. She never moved a muscle. She retired in glory and is still my beloved friend and teacher.

"The dog with whom I currently compete, Hawksmoor Sissel (Cammie), was the beneficiary of all that Alix taught me and consequently is an exceptionally focused, extremely happy worker. We are currently competing at Open level, and, hopefully, will continue through Utility level.

"If you think that Obedience is an activity you might enjoy, take advantage of your pup's natural instinct to pick up and carry things by encouraging him to pick up the dumb-bell and glove required for Obedience work. Enroll in a puppy training class emphasizing positive reinforcement. Build a loving, positive relationship with your Lab and make being near you a fun, rewarding place to be."

Hawksmoor Sissel ("Cammie"): a happy and focused worker.

- After you have taken about 10 steps, circle your hand, luring your Lab to turn, say "Heel" and now the two of you begin to walk forward.
- Again, reward with a treat every few steps, especially if he glances in your direction.
- As your Lab gains confidence that he won't bump into anything, in small increments, begin to raise the treat to your waist. You will still be rewarding with a treat every few steps, but the treat will now come from waist height.
- Gradually add more steps before giving the treat, until your Lab will walk with you for short distances, say 20 yards (18 meters).
- Be sure to give your Lab breaks for sniffing and exploring.
- Do two or three short heelwork sessions during the course of a 30-minute stroll.

Then take the show on the road! Go to your local park or playground and begin the whole process from the first step. This repetition is critical because your Lab has learned this only in your backyard so far. He may not yet know that the word "Heel" means the same thing in a different location. Lower your expectations in any new environment, beginning each session with the first step. By the third or fourth new environment, your Labrador will know that "Heel" means the same thing no matter where he is. This would be true for every exercise you teach your dog.

Gradually introduce changes of pace and changes of direction as your Lab becomes more proficient.

FREESTYLE

Canine Freestyle is dancing for dogs. It is derived from traditional Obedience moves, but set to music. A relatively recent phenomenon in Britain (where it is commonly known as Heelwork to Music) and in the U.S. (referred to by its more popular name of Canine Freestyle), "dog dancing" has a much longer pedigree in Canada, where it first originated.

"Dog dancing is growing in popularity all the time"

The sport has only existed in the U.K. and the U.S. since the early 1990s. Despite its infancy, it is growing in popularity all the time. However, its youth means that it has not yet achieved official recognition by either the Kennel Club of England or the American Kennel Club.

Canada's longer Freestyle tradition, and the fact that Freestyle is recognized there as an official competitive event, has resulted in Canadian criteria being used as the basis for Freestyle competition in America and Britain. However, these are guidelines only. There is little in the way of set routines, hence its popular name, Freestyle.

Performance length depends on which organization is hosting the event. In the U.K., the average performance length is around three to four minutes, whereas in the U.S. there is more flexibility, with performances lasting between two and six minutes. So long as the

DISCO FEVER

Peggy Phelps from Midlothian, Texas, has been practicing Canine Freestyle for four years. Here she describes how she got started, and how she and her Labrador, War, have formed a partnership to rival Fred Astaire and Ginger Rogers.

"I had heard of Canine Freestyle but didn't know much about it until I attended a two-day Canine Freestyle seminar back in July 1995," says Peggy. "I was hooked. In November of the same year I entered my first competition.

"I originally started with a Shetland Sheepdog who danced to the *Watermelon Crawl*. This was because War was still very young, and not ready for the demands of Freestyle. I still perform with my Sheltie, but I now work mainly with War because he enjoys it so much.

"War was born six years ago. His name may sound aggressive, but you couldn't ask for a more friendly and responsive dog. His mother's name was Sabre, and his full name is Sabre's War Lord. We named him that because almost from day one he was lording it over the other puppies. He seemed much more intelligent and forward. I knew I would have to keep him. Now that he is fully grown, the name fits him like a glove. He is built just like a warlord—85 lbs. in weight and 25 in. tall.

"We progressed to Competitive Obedience and some Agility training. War had no difficulties with Obedience, and the time was right for a new challenge. I started to teach him a few simple turns. He took to it immediately. I remember teaching him to spin, which was one of the first moves I ever taught him, and he was almost perfect the first time. Some people use toys to motivate their dog, but with War it was simply a case of 'Follow that Treat!'. All I had to do was move the treat correctly and War did the rest.

"War is a Lab that loves to be close to people. This character trait can be used to good effect when performing lateral moves. His enthusiasm and wagging tail as he bounds towards me is really special. For reverse moves, it took a little more training and a lot more patience. War is such a big dog that he found this quite difficult at first, but he's got the hang of it now.

War is lord of the dance floor.

"War seems to like certain songs more than others. If he really likes a piece of music he will get very excited. One of his favorites is *Boogie Fever*, which we perform quite often at demonstrations. Once you have chosen the song, the rest follows easily.

"If you listen to the music long enough, routines start appearing in your mind. Get the dog involved as well. War has a habit of upsetting my carefully thought out script, and improvising with his own moves. Ordinarily, I don't mind this. If War has chosen the move, he is probably happier performing that rather than one of my routines. It can be a bit daunting if he does his own thing in the middle of a competition, but I just have to keep my head and work with him, rather than trying to force him back to the script. After all, this is supposed to be fun for the dog.

"I remember one event in Houston where the audience was enormous. I was really nervous, although War didn't seem in the least bit fazed. Well, we got out there, got in our starting positions, took a deep breath, waited for the music to start... and it was the wrong track. My life flashed before my eyes. I thought War would hate it and run away. As it turned out, he just looked at me, jumped up, put his paws in my jacket pockets, and sort of started waltzing with me until they put on the right track. Then it was business as usual. We had a standing ovation at the end of it—the audience simply went wild.

"War truly understands the meaning of showmanship. When he is out there in front of an audience he hams it up for all it's worth. It's pure entertainment.

"The costumes are an important part of a performance. When we go out and do *Boogie Fever*, our costumes are amazing. I wear spangly white trousers and a white jacket, with a black shirt and white bow-tie. War wears a bow-tie too. We look as if we are a duo, rather than some mad woman who's only brought her dog along for the ride!"

choice of music falls within the specified timeframe, competitors are allowed to dance to any tune they choose.

Ring size is usually an average of about 13 by 26 yards (12 by 24 meters), although this varies across venues. In all cases there is ample space for any moves the handler (or for that matter an enterprising and improvising canine partner) can envisage.

Although there are no set routines or judging criteria, points are usually awarded on the basis of Technical Execution (degree of difficulty, dog/handler precision) and Artistic Impression (choreography, costume, synchronization, etc.). In particular, judges look for the degree of accord between dog and handler, and evidence that the dog is enjoying himself. Also important is the ease with which the dog responds to verbal cues. From a spectator's or a judge's perspective, a performance should not be broken up with verbal commands, but should be dominated by the music and a well-executed routine. It should look as if the dog and handler really are dancing.

FLYBALL

Flyball is fun, fast, and furious. It involves two long, narrow courses parallel to each other, each consisting of four hurdles, at the end of which is a box that releases a tennis ball when triggered. Two four-dog teams compete against each other in a doggie relay race. Each member must race up to the box, trigger it, catch the ball, and return back over the jumps before the next team member can start the course. The winning team is the one that completes the course in the

IN THE FAST LANE

Jean Sloman became involved in Flyball when she realized her working Lab needed something to keep him occupied. Black Lab Freddie was originally Jean's husband's guide dog, but he was retired at the age of four.

"Freddie retired not long after my husband, Alan, and I moved to a new town. Where we lived before, Alan would walk to work, but when we moved, Alan had to get to work by train. At first Freddie loved the new challenge and worked very well, but after a while it became apparent that all was not well and Freddie began to work slowly. It was through a process of elimination that Alan discovered that it was his route to work that Freddie was unhappy about. When Alan was dressed in his shirt and tie, ready for work, Freddie was reluctant to go. However, when Alan was dressed in casual clothes, on weekends, Freddie was eager and willing. Alan found that trains were the real cause of Freddie's stress; in fact after a while Freddie tried to avoid the train station altogether. After a lot of help and guidance from Guide Dogs for the Blind Association, sadly there was no alternative but to retire him.

Freddie flies over the hurdles.

"We had the option of keeping Freddie, and because I only work part-time, and I can take Freddie with me, we decided to keep him. There was a transition period before Alan got his new guide dog, and, during this time, we worked to get Freddie bonded more closely to me. I would feed him, take him out, and he would spend more time with me. When Jason, Alan's new guide dog, came along, it didn't come as so much of a shock to Freddie, as he had weaned himself on to me. Although he would sometimes want to guide Alan, he was quite relieved that, when Alan was wearing a suit, he didn't have to take him to work on the train any more.

"Because Freddie was retired, I wanted to find something else he could do. He is a working type, and is very active. And he loves tennis balls. He was quite content in his retirement, but I felt he needed to use his brain more. I considered Agility, but a few people suggested we try Flyball. I had never even heard of it before, but I went along to a local show where some competitions were being held.

"As soon as I saw Flyball, I knew Freddie would love it. He's a very lively Lab and likes to be busy. I don't know much about Agility or Obedience, but from a spectator's point of view, Flyball is much more exciting as you can see who is winning. You can watch Agility and think 'Oh, that dog did well,' and then it won't be placed. You need to know the intricacies of the sport.

"I spoke to some of the Flyball people at the show, and, by pure coincidence, there was a club very near to me, so we joined. Freddie took to it really quickly. The way it was taught was brilliant—everything was done stage by stage, nothing was rushed.

"Although Freddie isn't as nimble as a Collie, he is slim and athletic, and is a very fast mover. He is so obsessed with tennis balls that he is very motivated. To keep him focused we sometimes restrict his access to tennis balls outside training, but I doubt he will ever become bored with them. We have to watch him when we go out walking, because if he sees other dogs playing with a ball, he will be off. His recall is very good, so we can call him anyway, but we do have to keep an eye on him.

"In training, we were taught about 'secondary motivators'. These are used once the dog has the ball, and you need to motivate him to return to you just as quickly. It's the same as if you throw a ball for a dog in the park. He'll race off to get it, but will bring it back slowly, because he already has what he wants—there's no need for him to rush. I tried using food as a secondary motivator, but Freddie wasn't interested. The only thing that worked was another tennis ball! On his return run from the box, I now wave another tennis ball at him to speed him up, and when he gets to me, he carries them both in his mouth. He's just nutty for tennis balls!

"After about three months we were ready to compete, and at the first competition we came second. He has had many successes since. I'm very proud of him, and he loves it. When he goes to Flyball, he's a different dog. He bounces around and barks—he's like a wild child. I'm just so pleased we managed to find something for him to enjoy."

fastest time. If a dog drops the ball or knocks over a hurdle, he must run the course again once the last team member has finished.

Unlike Obedience, where considerable precision is required, Flyball allows the dog to really let his hair down, and compete flat-out. Because speed and agility are key factors at competition level, it is often the working type of Labrador that is particularly successful, though other types (i.e., stockier show types) still have great fun taking part. As well as having a build better suited to Flyball work, working Labs also seem more focused on the tennis ball.

As well as making sure your dog is suitable for Flyball (some dogs just don't take to it), you have to be prepared to put in some hard work, too. Flyball is all about teamwork—between you and your dog, and you and the other handlers. Your dog might give his very best performance, but if you are responsible for a late changeover (where one dog races to the finishing line, just as the next dog starts his run), you can let the whole team down. If you are competitive, have some hours to spare, enjoy teamwork and the company of other dogs and people, it may well be the canine sport for you.

TRACKING

In Britain, tracking is tested as part of Working Trials (a sport which also features Obedience and Agility skills). In America, tracking is a sport in itself. So what is "tracking?" It is a vigorous, non-competitive outdoor sport that tests the dog's ability to recognize and follow human scent. This skill is very useful and is used by the police force and by search and rescue organizations.

The "track" is a pre-plotted course walked by a "tracklayer"—someone that the dog doesn't know. The length of the track, the number of turns in it, and the length of time it has been allowed to age vary according to the test's level of difficulty. A flag indicates the beginning of the track, and an additional flag placed about 30 yards (27 meters) from the starting point indicates the direction in which the track has been laid. A leather article such as a glove is dropped to signal the end of the track.

The handler has no previous knowledge regarding the direction of the track. He starts his dog in the direction indicated by the flag and follows at least 20 feet (6 meters) behind his dog. The dog wears a nonrestrictive harness to which a long line is attached. The dog must follow the track closely, make each turn appropriately, and indicate the article at the end either by lying or sitting next to it, or retrieving it.

Tracking is an intensely challenging sport. The sense of reward upon completing a track successfully is great, and the sport really shows how closely humans and dogs can work together. Be warned—once you've tried it, you could fast become hooked!

With the Labrador's amazing sense of smell, tracking comes as second nature.

ON THE RIGHT TRACK

Linda Strauch from Reading, Pennsylvania, has been tracking for 10 years. Rorie (Misty Glen's Rif Aroara), is her third tracking dog.

"Rorie and I had done Obedience work, and I considered tracking as an additional activity for a change of pace (Agility and Flyball had not yet gained their present popularity). Although there are now other fun and competitive activities in which my dog and I have found a great deal of pleasure, I continue to track because it is a wonderful confidence-builder and a great bonding tool. It is one of the few canine sports in which you must trust your dog to make the decisions. While the sport does require a commitment of time and effort, most people truly enjoy spending time outside with their dogs, and we have developed a wonderful, non-competitive sense of camaraderie.

"Although tracking is often started alone, eventually someone else is needed to lay a track. Good tracklayers are hard to find and are to be cherished. I have had the good fortune to find some really special ones—ones who will go out in all kinds of weather, lay tracks wearing trashbags because they forgot their raincoats. And there are other ones that will leave articles of clothing because they forgot to bring a glove and your dog *has* to find something at the end.

"Labs are natural trackers. They were bred to work closely with their owners, to be biddable, and to retrieve birds that do not always land in open ground. Dogs have an amazing sense of smell, and I never tire of watching their joy when they discover that you actually want them to smell the ground and come up with something.

"My latest tracking dog and I earned our TD title two years ago. Our track was laid on a lovely open grassy field. It was a crisp fall day, slightly overcast—perfect tracking conditions. However, no one mentioned that, until fairly recently, the area had been inhabited by dairy cows. My girl completed her track in seven minutes from start to finish—never missing a beat or turn—and managed to enjoy the wonderful treats (known locally as "meadow muffins") that her bovine friends had left her. Of course, she considered for just a millisecond how wonderful having a roll in that great stuff would be, but changed her mind after briefly lowering one shoulder and getting a gentle reminder of why she was out there.

"She reached the end of the course and retrieved the glove, all smiles and tail-waggly (as only Labs can be), promptly offered it to the tracklayer as if to say, 'Excuse me, did you drop this?' Needless to say, she was considered the most entertaining dog of the day. So typical of a Lab to get the job done with panache and humor!

"To get started with tracking, first get and read an official rule book. There are also several good books on the subject. Many Obedience clubs hold tracking days where they demonstrate the sport. Some areas have tracking clubs. A word of warning though—it can be addictive for both humans and canines!"

Misty Glen's Rif Aroara ('Rorie').

SHOWING

Being the most popular breed of dog, it comes as no surprise that Labrador classes have huge entries, so showing can be rather intimidating for the novice. With so many excellent (and sometimes not so excellent) dogs in the ring, it can be difficult to do well, but if you have an outstanding dog, he will be noticed, no matter how many others he is competing against. Large entries benefit the breed overall, as it means only the very best of the best go on to win.

Getting Started

The most important aspect of successful showing is, obviously, to have a good dog. Read as many books as you can, and look at many photos of different dogs. Visit Championship shows and talk to breeders. Before getting a dog, you need to establish the type you prefer. Generally, show Labradors tend to be heavier in build than their working counterparts, but you need to look at heads, colors, and general conformation, and select a line that you like the look of.

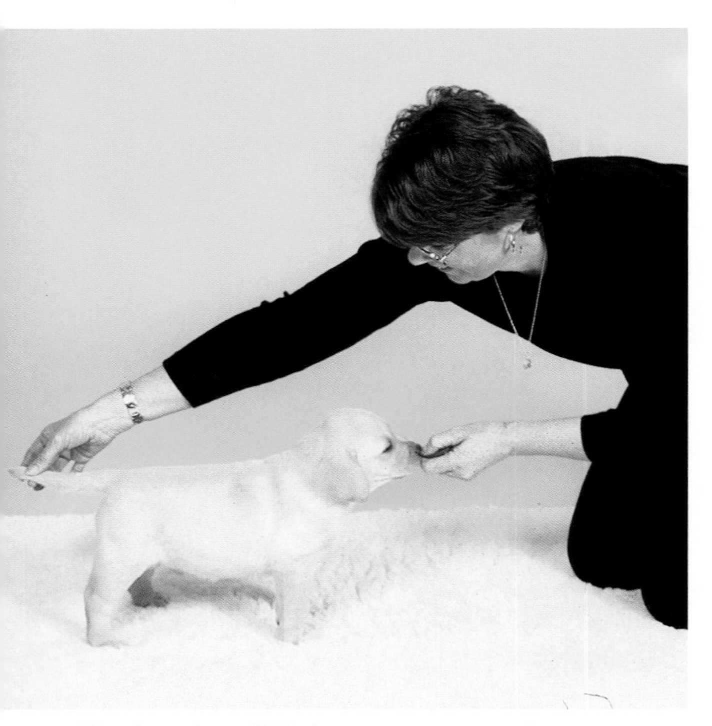

The breeder will help you to assess show potential.

Once you are sure of your preferred type, talk to as many people as possible to get recommendations as to the best breeders who specialize in the type of Labrador you want.

Talk to the breeder when the litter is born and explain that you would like a show dog. The breeder will then be able to pick a pup with the best potential. Note the word "potential." All the best breeding in the world is not necessarily a guarantee of a sure winner. If only showing were so simple! Be prepared for some disappointments—perhaps your Labrador, despite the best parental hip scores, will have a high score, rendering him or her useless as future breeding stock; perhaps your dog will develop cow hocks or simply will not enjoy showing, and so will lack the all-important "ring presence." As our case history on page 80 shows, competing in the ring is just half the battle—getting there in the first place, with the right dog, can be a struggle in itself.

Assessing Your Dog

You may have bought a Labrador, and as he matures, you think he may be worth showing. The best advice is to talk to breed experts to see if your dog really has a chance of making a show career for himself. You do not want to waste your time and money entering shows where you will just be laughed out of the ring.

If you are told your dog isn't the right standard for the show ring, do not be too disappointed. The most important thing is that he is a good family pet, and in your eyes he will always be the most beautiful dog in the world—whatever anyone else thinks. Be realistic, and perhaps consider "fun" shows instead. They are just as enjoyable and offer a good day out for all the family.

If you are adamant that you want to take up showing at a serious level, then you may have to consider starting from scratch and taking on another dog.

Home Practice

From the time your Labrador is a puppy, spend just a few minutes every day getting him in the correct position. This is particularly important as Labradors are expected to free-stand (i.e., no stacking).

- Put your Lab in the correct position—four-square, with his head up, and tail approximately level with his topline.
- Say "Stand," wait a moment, then reward him with praise and a tiny taste of a treat.
- Be observant—give the command and a treat whenever you see him standing correctly—whether he is standing beside you in the kitchen while you are peeling carrots, or gets in front of the television while your favorite program is on.

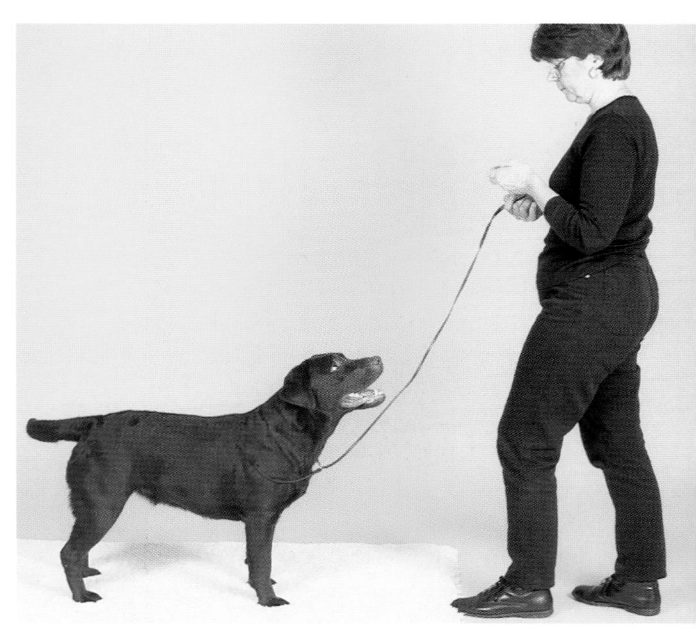

The Labrador must learn to stand in show pose.

The Labrador's love of food means he will quickly catch on to what is going on, and you will probably find him striking show poses all over the place—in the hope of earning an extra treat!

When you know your Labrador understands what "Stand" means and the position required, you can gradually wean him off the treats, so that you give a treat only when he holds the pose longer and better than before.

Eventually, you can give treats only when you want the very best performance in a show situation. Some judges do not like the use of treats in the ring, but most recognize that it gets the best out of the dog.

You can always try *pretending* you have a treat in your hand, but this doesn't wash with some Labs, and if they realize you don't *really* have a treat, there's every chance they will lose their

Like many people in the ring, Kevin and Julie Barrett from Poole, England, came to showing from a pet background. After Toby, their 11-year-old pet Labrador, died, Julie and Kevin missed the companionship of a dog and decided to purchase another. They chose Jasper, a black Labrador.

"We met up with a breeder, who introduced us to some more people in the breed," explains Julie. "Our first impression was that it was very strange to see so many people spend their spare time that way. As we sat and watched some classes it was fascinating—seeing all the different colors, sizes, and types of Labradors was really interesting.

"We bought a show potential puppy, Sophie, but she turned out to be too big and did not like to show. Sophie still lives with us as a pet. We decided to get another dog to show. Pickle won a few puppy classes, but when she was tested at a year old it showed she had a high hip score, which meant we could not breed from her. We decided to rehouse her with someone in the family, so we still get to see her a lot.

"We then got Cher, who came from a well-known lady in the breed. Cher was Joint Top Winning Labrador Puppy 1995 and we consider her to be our foundation bitch. When the time was right, we decided to mate her to a stud dog that we liked who had a good hip score, a clear eye certificate, and who was a good example of the breed.

"Picking which pup we would keep from Sophie's litter was easy. Spike (Rumpole's Gold of Poolebar) stood out from the beginning. Friends in the breed would come around, and, without any prompting from us, would immediately pick out Spike, and say 'Oh, he's

Spike: competing against the top dogs in the show ring today.

nice'. There was something about him. He stood four-square, legs planted properly, head up, tail in the right position, but there was also a real presence and charisma about him.

"We entered classes at Open and Championship shows; he won many puppy classes in his breed at Open shows and was placed at Championship shows. He then went on to win classes at Championship shows, one of which qualified him for Crufts. His mother, Cher, has a studbook number, and this qualifies her for Crufts every year, but with Spike it was different. Cher had come from someone else, but we qualified Spike for Crufts all by ourselves. It was a very nice feeling.

"It was my husband, Kevin, that handled Spike in the Crufts ring. I had had an operation that meant I couldn't handle Spike for a while, and Spike and Kevin had built up such a close bond that it seemed a shame to interrupt it. I watched from the sidelines.

"There were 26 in the ring and it was nerve-wracking for Kevin, who was wondering whether Spike would behave, or whether he would jump up (some do!). Spike was lucky enough to get through to the second round. Even though we didn't get placed, it was still a great experience to be at Crufts with our dog.

"It has been tough getting this far. When you first start, you look at everything through rose-colored glasses, and think everything will be hunky-dory and that you will come away with a nice rosette at the end of the day, but it isn't like that. As we have shown, there can be lots of downs just getting started.

"Despite this, we really enjoy showing. It's a good day out. You can pick up lots of tips from people in the breed. We have made lots of friends, and have met people from all walks of life and from different countries. There's a real sense of camaraderie, and at the end of the day you always go home with the nicest dog!"

motivation, and will not show to their best ability. See if yours is trusting enough to be fooled by the "pretend treat" trick—but be sure not to overdo it. You must give sufficient treats so that, when you pretend you have one, and simply hold your hand up, your Lab thinks there is one there. If you never give treats, then he will never believe you when you pretend you have one, and will get very frustrated.

Ring Training

Ring-training classes are very useful. They will show you and your Labrador what you can expect in the ring, and you can pick up tips and advice from more experienced show hands. Your sociable Labrador will find them great fun, mixing with many different breeds, and the experience will help him to become well socialized with other dogs. He will also learn to accept being handled and assessed by strangers, in anticipation of the judging procedure in the ring.

One of the most important factors is that your Lab will learn to concentrate and Stand, without always wanting to play with the other dogs. (At least, that's the theory—in practice, puppy classes can be mayhem, but most dogs grow out of it once the novelty has worn off.)

Entering Shows

When you feel you and your dog are ready to enter your first show, scan the dog press for details of future shows, and request schedules for those that you are interested in.

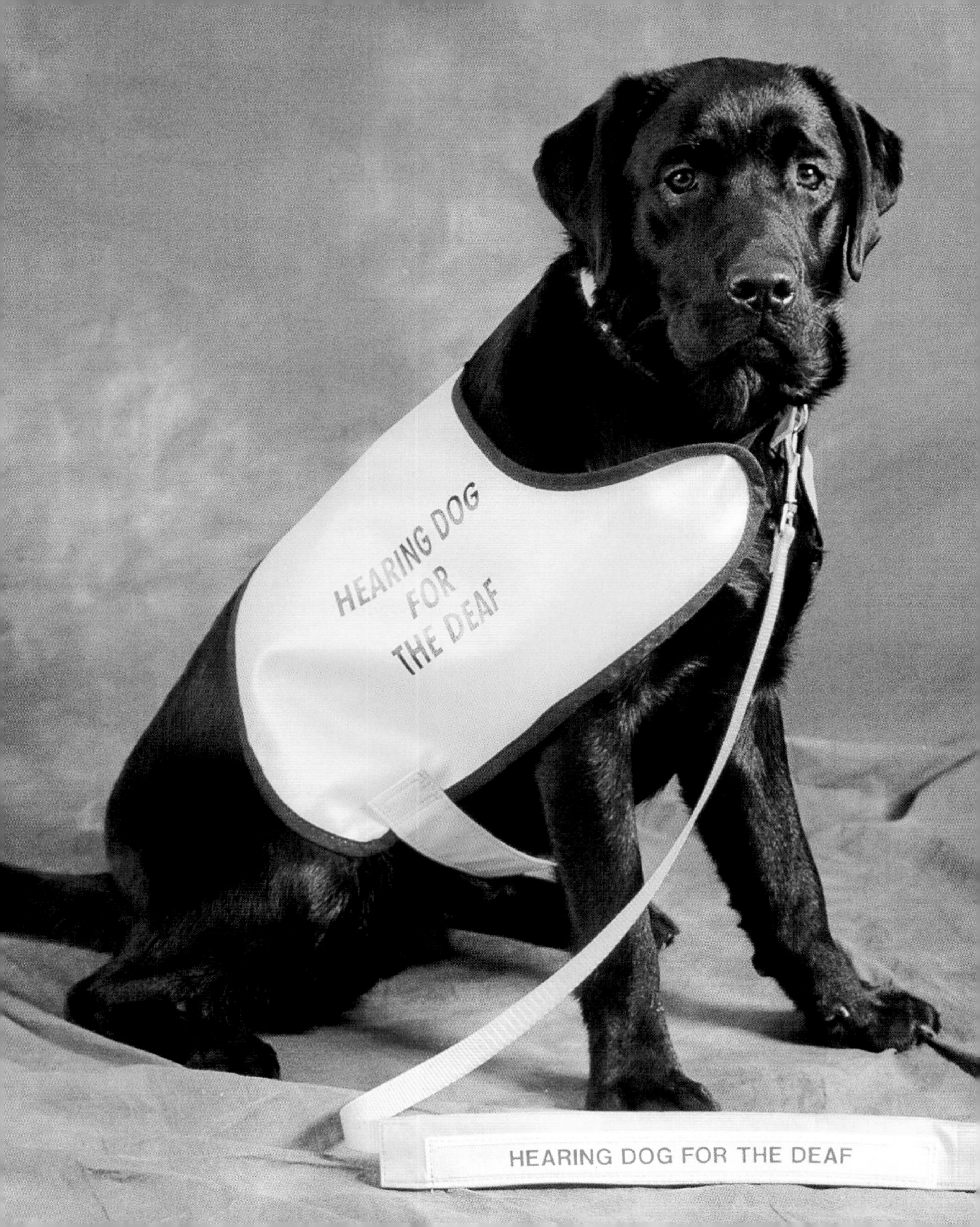
HEARING DOG
FOR
THE DEAF
HEARING DOG FOR THE DEAF

CHAPTER SIX

A SPECIAL BOND

The Labrador's gundog background lends itself well to a variety of jobs in the assistance of man. As a sniffer dog, detecting explosives (for the police and army), drugs (for the police and customs officials), or accelerants (for the fire service), the Labrador's sensitive nose and love of hunting smells is invaluable. Other gundog breeds are also used, particularly the Springer Spaniel, but a well-trained, well-motivated Lab is an asset to any handler.

The Lab is also pre-programmed as a worker—he loves to be busy. This healthy work ethic makes him a welcome recruit to sniffer dog work.

Sniffer Dogs

Every year, sniffer dogs find substantial drug hauls, sometimes worth millions. To the dog, however, his crucially important job is just one big game. The dogs are trained to find a toy—it can be anything, but at the outset of training it is usually a piece of thick plastic tubing. The tubing contains drugs, and has holes for the scent to escape. The tube is secured so that the drugs cannot be reached by the dog.

When the dog finds the "toy" with the drug's scent, or gives an indication that he knows where it is, he is rewarded by getting the toy to play with.

Food treats are never used. Not only will it encourage the dog to scavenge (searching for crumbs instead of drugs), there is also the danger that the dog could ingest something that has drugs concealed inside it.

There are two types of sniffer dog—the passive response detector dog that is used to detect drugs on people and will then react in a passive manner (e.g., sit quietly) when a substance has been found; and a proactive response detector dog, which will search freight vehicles, ships, etc., and will usually scratch or dig at the source of the scent when he finds something.

LABS NOSE BEST

Chris Terry, a Dual Drug Detector Dog Handler from Southampton, England, is one of only two handlers in Customs and Excise that has both a passive and proactive dog. In his seven years with the dog unit, he has had eight dogs, and one of his current canine colleagues is Jet, a Labrador-Collie cross. He has also had Springers, a German Shorthaired Pointer, and two purebred Labradors—Jack and Rocky.

I've always been into animals, and had pets at home," says Chris. "As far as I'm concerned, I have the best job, at this level, in Customs and Excise.

Chris Terry with Jet.

"The dogs we use tend to be from rescue shelters or are donated by members of the public—we do not have our own breeding program. The dogs usually start training between the ages of 18 and 36 months. They have to display certain characteristics before being accepted into training—they have to be people-friendly, agile, not noise-shy, and have low body-sensitivity. They must be keen, show drive, and enjoy hunting and searching.

"The majority of the dogs we use are Springer Spaniels. Because they are smaller, they can get into tighter spaces than Labradors can. However, what the Labrador loses in size, he more than makes up for in other areas. He is keen, enthusiastic, and determined, and manages to get into most gaps.

"Smugglers obviously don't want us to find their drugs, so they hide them as carefully as possible. Our dogs are trained on four main substances—cannabis, heroin, cocaine, and amphetamines. Cannabis is the most easily scented drug, whereas heroin has the smallest 'scent picture'. Smugglers will wrap the drugs in coffee, onions, etc., and hide them in boxes, or within their vehicles. If a dog just skirts by, he will have a reduced chance of finding something—he has to be very thorough.

"Passive detector dogs have a particularly hard job. For example, at an airport, the dogs will walk past passengers leaving a plane. If someone has concealed drugs by swallowing them in condoms, the dog doesn't have much of a chance of finding them. He can detect the smell if they have dropped a little on their clothes, though, or if they sweat or break wind.

"Jack, my first Labrador, once found 304 lbs. (138 kg) of cannabis when working with me. It was concealed in the roof lining of a freight vehicle. The vehicle contained frozen goods, and the temperature inside was minus 20 degrees. Obviously, such conditions suppressed the scent. Jack inspected inside but couldn't find anything. However, when checking the outside of the vehicle, he kept pacing backward and forward. I knew he was restless—you learn to notice even the most subtle differences in your dog's behavior. This can only come from repeated training.

"Anyway, I knew Jack could smell something but that he was finding it hard to track down. One of the key pointers is if you call your dog and he doesn't come. Then you know that he'd rather have his toy than be with you. On further inspection of the vehicle, the drugs were found—thanks to Jack.

A sniffer dog showing passive response.

"He did a similar job another time when he found 55 lbs. (25 kg) of cannabis in the roof space of a truck unit (which pulls freight trailers). It was a cold, wet night, and when Jack got to the forward end of the trailer, he put his head up in the air. This is always a good sign, and I knew he was checking a scent he had picked up on. He jumped up to where the trailer hooked on to the truck, and stood on his two back legs, looking at the top of it. I couldn't have asked for a clearer indication. I passed the information on to the local officers, and they found the drugs.

"I've worked with several different breeds, but I prefer working with the Labrador. He operates differently to the Springer, but this difference can be an asset in some circumstances. For example, the Springer Spaniel can be a little manic. Springers look busy, but can be scatterbrains. The Labrador works at a steadier pace, which I prefer.

"Sometimes a Springer can race past a scent, then suddenly detect it, and quickly turn around. This can often be an excellent indication to the presence of drugs. However, sometimes, they work so quickly they can miss it altogether, and race through the scent picture so fast that they don't pick anything up!

"I like the temperament of the Labrador. For me, they are more relaxed, laid-back, and not so hyper. There's just something about them... they are affectionate and friendly. If my home circumstances changed and I was able to give a good home to a dog, I would definitely have a pet Lab."

ASSISTANCE DOGS

If you were to ask a member of the public what dogs were used as assistance dogs, most would reply, without hesitation, "The Labrador." Although many other breeds are used as guide dogs for the blind, hearing dogs for the deaf, and dogs for the disabled, it is the Labrador that seems to have monopolized this niche.

Producing an assistance dog is a science. Only the very best dogs are used, and intensive socializing and training goes into each one. With puppies, organizations usually have a puppy-walker program, where volunteers provide a home for the potential assistance dog for the first year of his life, socializing him thoroughly, and giving him an excellent grounding for his working adult life, where he is likely to face many situations usually foreign to many pet dogs.

The assistance dog charities assess the dogs throughout their lives, and the results are clear: Labs (and Lab crosses) can make excellent workers and companions. They are intelligent, respond well to training, and, most importantly, bond closely with their handlers. These qualities are essential for a successful partnership, as we will see in the following case histories.

GUIDE DOGS

The Labrador is the most popular pedigree dog used in guide dog work, and Labrador-Golden Retriever crosses are also used extensively. This wasn't always the case. When the guide dog movement first started (to help those wounded in World War I), German Shepherd Dogs were the chosen breed in Germany, Britain, and America.

Experiments with different breeds soon showed the Labrador had many of the qualities needed for a successful guide dog, and his keen working ability and amenable temperament made him an ideal choice for many owners.

"The Labrador is the most popular pedigree assistance dog"

Although the German Shepherd is still used for guide dog work, he needs a particular type of owner—a very confident handler, and one who can keep up with his faster walking pace. Incredibly adaptable and easy-going, the Labrador is not a "complicated" breed. He wears his heart on his sleeve, and suits many different owners and environments.

Guide Dogs for the Blind Association has recognized the following breed strengths:

- A friendly, willing, and pleasant disposition.
- Easy coat care.
- Reaches maturity sooner than some other breeds.

Guide Dogs of America is another fan of the breed, saying the Labrador has a good health and temperament record. A spokesperson for the charity says the Lab "is a strong dog, and easy to maintain. He isn't as jumpy as the Golden—he's more easy-going, and is not as easily distracted."

GET UP AND GO – WITH FREEMONT

Frank Pavolillo from Imperial Beach, California, can testify to the breed's many qualities. Frank has lived and worked with Freemont, a very pale yellow Labrador, for five years. Freemont is Frank's first guide dog, acquired after he developed tunnel vision and limited sight as a result of sugar diabetes.

"When I first lost my vision, I didn't want to go anywhere or do anything," says Frank. "I just wanted to sit at home. For someone who has been on the go all his life, it was rough. But my wife, Lorraine, had other plans, and made me go to a center for the blind. All the instructors were blind, and I thought 'If they can do it, so can I'.

"I went into mobility training, and was taught to walk with a cane at quite a fast pace, but it wasn't for me. Some people like it, some don't. It got me out of the house for the first time in a long time, but it has its limitations. One day I was out walking and I swiped the cane to the right, then to the left, but the cane didn't show there was an uncovered water meter coming up—and I didn't realize until I stepped in it. A guide dog sees everything. If I had been with Freemont, he would have walked me to the left or to the right of the hole. A dog is also a safety-catch when crossing the road, and might see or hear something you can't—a cane can't do that. Plus, a cane can't be a friend to you.

"The bond I have with Freemont is tremendous. People say he watches me all the time. He lays at my feet and doesn't take his eyes off me.

Frank Pavolillo with guide dog Freemont.

"I have always loved dogs, and also have a pet Labrador cross—Duchess—who is 16. Before that, I had a German Shepherd who was put to sleep at 18 years.

"Duchess was a little jealous when Freemont first came home with me, and would try to get the upper hand over him, but they worked their problems out. Now, if Freemont and I have been to guide dog training school for two or three days, when we get back Duchess is so happy to see us both; she will really let rip, running around and playing with her pal. With Freemont, she's just like a young dog again.

"Old age has had some effect on Duchess, though, and she has started to lose her vision. Freemont senses this, and guides her around if she's a bit lost—nudging her into the right place.

"Freemont's on a strict diet at the moment. He's a typical Lab, and if Duchess leaves some of her food, Freemont finishes it off for her. And when we go out, people just want to give him food all the time. Apart from that, I haven't had any problems with him.

"With Freemont, I get out more—I have my freedom. If I want, I can just grab him, put the harness on, catch a bus and go into town. No problems. I can do anything I want. Some people say to me 'Are you sure you're blind?', and I say 'I ought to know!'"

HEARING DOGS

Everyone is familiar with the work of guide dogs, but fewer people know of the work that dogs can do for the deaf. Being deaf or having only partial hearing presents its own difficulties—some mundane, some life-threatening. Hearing dogs act as their owners' ears, alerting them to many sounds, from the front-door bell, alarm clock, and cooking timer, to fire or smoke alarms.

Claire Guest is National Operations Director for Hearing Dogs for Deaf People, based in Oxfordshire in the U.K. She explains why the charity uses so many Labradors.

"The Labrador is an adaptable dog who copes with varying situations and family life. His trainable, sociable nature makes him an ideal companion both in social situations and when working to sounds. The Labrador alerts reliably

A NEW SENSE OF FREEDOM

Samantha Johnson began to go deaf when she was still in her teens. Now severely deaf, she describes how her yellow Labrador, Sage, has made her deafness less of a disability.

"People often don't realize that I am nearly completely deaf. I can lip-read well and because I did not start to go deaf until I was in my teens, when I talk I don't sound like a deaf speaker. I cannot hear any sounds of a high frequency, and only a very limited range of sounds in a middle frequency. Most of what I can hear is of a bass-level frequency. This is why I can use the telephone. It has been specially adapted to alter the voice of the other person and make it deeper, in order for me to hear it.

"It is not being able to hear the higher frequencies that has limited my life in the past. Things like not being able to hear the doorbell, the telephone, or the smoke alarm used to make me a bit anxious. It also meant that if I was expecting anyone, I would have to hover by the front door so that I could see them arrive rather than hear them. Having Sage has changed all of that.

"I found out about hearing dogs through my work as a hearing therapist. During one of my classes a lady turned up to give a talk about hearing dogs for the deaf. I wanted to find out more and eventually got approval to receive a hearing dog. I didn't know what type of dog I was going to get. All I said was that I wanted a medium or large-sized dog, as my husband and I like walking and would like the dog to accompany us.

"I was given Sage, and now I have so much more confidence. I actually like being at home on my own now, whereas before I would feel really worried and insecure. Now I know I am safe, as Sage will let me know immediately if anything happens—like the smoke alarm going off. He alerts me to the telephone and doorbell, which means I am able to get on with other things when I am home alone, just like a normal person.

"Sage absolutely loves his work as a hearing dog. He just laps up all the attention. I do a lot of fundraising work for charity, and Sage comes along with me. He tries to look as mournful as possible because people can't resist the temptation of coming over and giving him a pat or a biscuit in an effort to cheer him up.

"One of his favorite haunts is my hairdresser's salon. All the regulars in there know him, and they lavish attention on him. He also likes going

to sounds, particularly as a food reward is used intermittently—the way to many of their hearts!"

DOGS FOR THE DISABLED

The work of an assistance dog is incredibly varied, and very much depends on the owner's individual disability. Dogs for the Disabled in the U.K. uses many Labradors, saying they are:

- Easy to maintain (minimum coat care, never fussy eaters).
- Gundogs, and so have a soft retrieve.
- Willing and responsive.
- A good size, so can do all the activities required.
- Have a good life expectancy (with a working life of 10–11 years).

Each dog for the disabled is trained specifically for its intended recipient. As everyone's disability

out shopping with me. Sage is such a magnificent dog to look at—really handsome. We get stopped a lot, particularly by children, who want to know more about him and how he helps me. Sage really likes children. I don't have any children of my own, but if I did, I know he would be brilliant with them."

According to Samantha, Sage is such an attraction she sometimes feels she fades into the background unnoticed. "One day I had a collection day outside my local shopping center. Behind me there was a banner with *Hearing Dogs for the Deaf* written on it. While I was there, a man came up to me and said: 'Oh! What a handsome dog. It's such a pity that he's deaf!', and he dropped some money into my collection tray. I replied: 'Actually, Sage isn't deaf at all, it's me who is deaf. Sage is specially trained to help me.' Most perturbed, the man retrieved his money from my collection tray and walked off. Obviously, he felt far more sympathy for the dog than he did for me!

"I will definitely have another hearing dog when Sage eventually retires—but, hopefully, he has lots of years left in him. He is a wonderful dog, and has given my life a freedom that I thought I had lost forever."

Sage: hearing dog for Samantha Johnson.

is different, so the dog's training must vary too. Each dog is trained on three main principles:

- Pull—pulling doors open, pulling socks off his owner, pulling laundry out of the washing machine, pulling an empty wheelchair to his owner, etc. All these "pull" exercises are an adaptation of a fun game with a tug-toy.
- Push—from his puppyhood the dog is taught to give his paw. This is adapted so the dog will touch a target in his trainer's hand. The target can then be moved to the floor, or the wall, etc., so that, eventually, the dog will be

ENDAL: DOG OF THE MILLENNIUM

Canine Partners for Independence is another organization that provides and trains assistance dogs for disabled people, and one of the charity's dogs, a Labrador named Endal, has become something of a superstar since he was named Dog of the Millennium for all the work he does for his owner, Allen Parton.

Allen, from Clanfield in Hampshire, U.K., thinks Endal more than deserves recognition for the way he has transformed his life.

"In 1991 I was serving with the Royal Navy in the Gulf War," he says. "Everything was going well and I was due to become an officer on my return. However, I was involved in a traffic accident, and sustained a serious head injury, resulting in me spending five years in the hospital.

"I came out fifty percent the man I was before. I am no longer mobile, and although I can use the right-hand side of my body, I have lost all feeling in it. I also lost my memory—I didn't know my wife or my children, and was psychologically very beaten up. I was intolerable at home. I sat in the corner, in my wheelchair, blaming everyone around me for what had happened. I was just awful to live with.

"One of my naval chums decided to give my wife and kids a break by taking me to America for a vacation, where I met some American war veterans with their assistance dogs. I returned home, and, by chance, my wife Sandra showed me a newspaper clipping about how Canine Partners for Independence needed puppy-walkers.

Endal: assistance dog for Allen Parton. Photo: Veronica Morgan CPI.

able to turn lights on and off, press elevator buttons and emergency alarms, and anything else indicated by his handler.

- Retrieve—again, this is treated like a game. The dog is rewarded for bringing back an item to his handler. This skill is very important and is used when the owner drops or cannot reach an item.

Dogs for the Disabled will then train the dog to perform a series of tasks. For example, a dog might be taught the following regime for dog walks—to open a cupboard, take out a lead, close it again, give it to the owner, fetch a coat, open the door, turn off the light, and close the door behind the owner.

"Sandra was approved and we took on six-week-old Ferdy, a yellow Labrador. I would go along with Sandra and Ferdy to some of their training sessions. I had a stutter, and so was always rude or gruff with people, and I would sit in the corner away from everyone else. It was my way of ensuring the stutter wasn't a problem—if I didn't have to communicate with anyone, my stutter didn't exist.

"I couldn't stay alone for long. Some of the dogs who were in their last six months of training kept coming up to me. One in particular, Endal, kept sitting with me and nudging me—trying to break through the armor I put up.

"I don't think anyone else could have got through to me. I was just so insular. Endal didn't look at my condition and think 'I can't be dealing with that', as some people did. He just kept offering me things, trying to be my friend. It was as if he knew there was a hurt there, and was determined to help.

"Eventually, Endal worked his way into my affections. Before this, I didn't know love or hate, happiness or sadness; I was a blob in a wheelchair. When the staff at Canine Partners for Independence saw how Endal and I had bonded, they suggested I apply for an assistance dog. At first I resented the thought. To me, an assistance dog was a badge of disability, but I wanted Endal, so I agreed.

Endal collects the mail.
Photo: Veronica Morgan CPI.

"I took Endal on a trial basis. I was frightened to give my all to him, knowing he could be taken away from me. But it was impossible not to love him.

HOME HELP

"That was two years ago. Endal is three now, and is my best friend. We share everything together. Endal watches me struggle with something, and leaps in to help out. One day, I was trying to get my card, money, and receipt out of an ATM. I went to move my chair closer to reach them, and Endal went right up and got them for me. I have even given him my card, with the arrow pointing the right way, and he has put it in the narrow slot for me. The first time he did it, there was a line of people behind us and they started applauding and cheering him!

"They say animals learn by repetition, but Endal doesn't—he just seems to know what I need. My day-to-day memory lasts just two days, and so my words for different items change all the time, but Endal still knows what I mean when I ask for something, even if I haven't used that word before. If I rub the side of my face, he knows I want to shave, and so gets my razor. And if I ask for my shoes, and I happen to have put them in the fridge or some other bizarre place, he finds them, no matter where they are.

"In the supermarket, I don't have to point to something I want. If I ask him to get me some brown sauce, he will find it—even if it's surrounded by red sauce or salad dressing. We are very much attuned to each other.

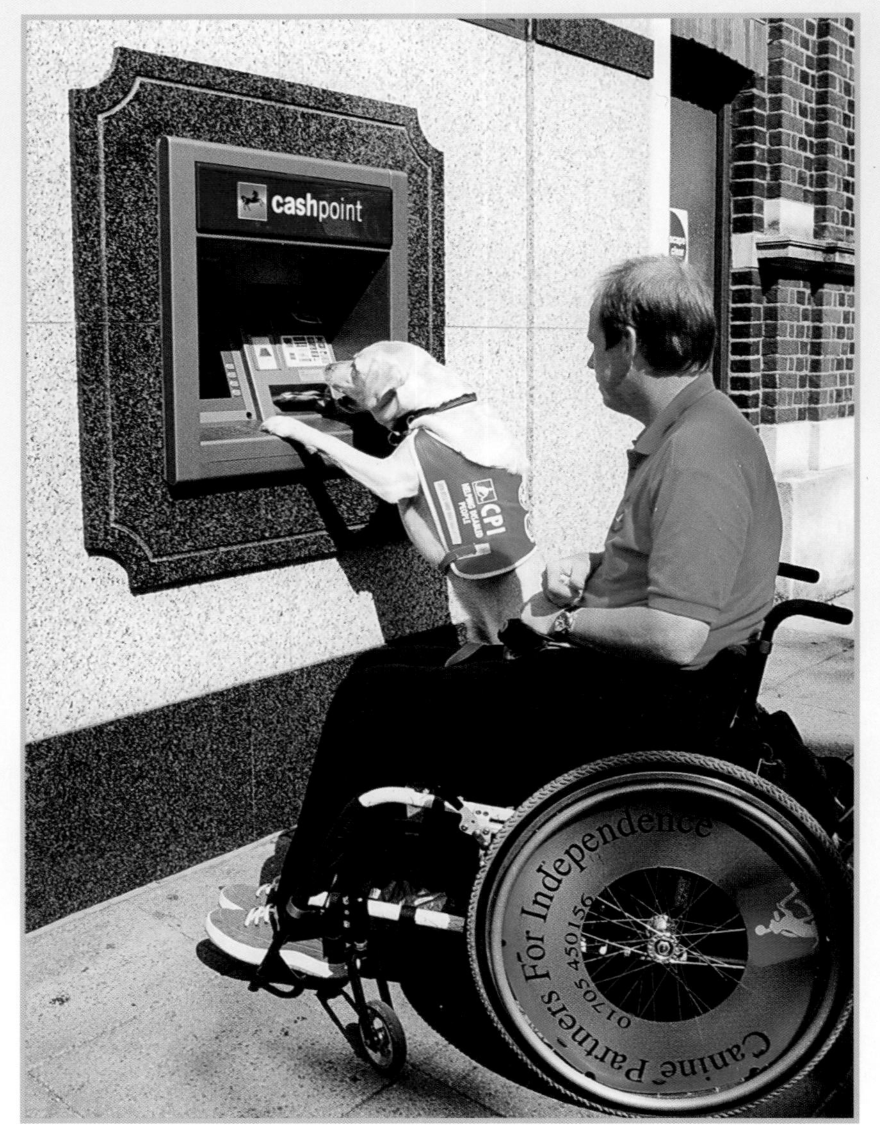

A quick learner, Endal works the cash dispenser. Photo: Veronica Morgan CPI.

MORALE BOOSTER

"Although Endal helps me physically, it is the psychological difference he has made to me that has changed my life. I am independent now. In fact Sandra has bought me a mobile phone so she can keep in touch with me!

"Sandra can leave me at home with Endal now, instead of being my full-time caregiver. If I collapse, Endal can put me in the recovery position, fetch a blanket and put it over me, and get help (either by bringing me the mobile phone and putting it next to my head, or by pressing my emergency alarm button). And if I forget to do something, Endal reminds me—especially if I forget to feed him at 5 P.M.! Typical Labrador!

"When I go to the pub, Endal rushes up to the bar and pays for the drinks. Most people walk into a pub alone, and come out of the pub alone. With Endal, everyone comes up and starts talking to us. The more I talk, the better my speech becomes, and the more my confidence grows. I can't even go to the shops without being stopped by people who want to talk about Endal.

"Being responsible for him has stopped me from being selfish. One day, Endal stood on something sharp and cut his pad. He got on my lap, distraught. I went to reach down for the telephone directory to call a vet, but I couldn't manage it. Endal saw I needed help, got off my lap, brought the directory to me, and got back on my lap. When the vet examined him, I went to give Endal a biscuit for being so good, but remembered they were in my bag, which I couldn't reach. Endal limped over to fetch the biscuit. The vet saw this and said 'I think he'll live!' Even though he was hurting, he still wanted to help me—and get a biscuit, of course!

"Sandra still puppy-walks for the charity. Having Endal around is great for the puppies as they see Endal fetching me things, and being rewarded, and they think it's normal. Sometimes Sandra will be brought the entire contents of a cupboard by a puppy—because they have seen Endal doing the same.

"I owe everything to Endal. I'm still married because of him. I have no memory, so I have to rebuild on a daily basis, but psychologically I am much improved. I'm no longer embittered. My children Liam (14) and Zoe (13) had lost their dad in the Gulf War; the man who came back was not the same as the one who sailed away. Endal brought us closer together again.

"Endal loves me for who I am. He makes me laugh no matter how I'm feeling. No other animal could have taught me emotion again."

Endal has given Allen back his independence. Photo: Veronica Morgan CPI.

QUEEN BEA

Bea, a six-year-old black Labrador, is incredibly popular with the elderly at the day hospital ward of the Royal Surrey Hospital in Guildford, U.K., where she visits with her owner, Tony Moyes.

"At the day hospital people have their blood pressure checked, and some have physiotherapy," says Tony, a police dog handler from Farnham, Surrey. "There's quite a community spirit there and they have a meal together. When I walk into the ward with Bea everyone is pleased to see the dog—and that's a very rewarding feeling. I sit down with them and they pat Bea, and we have a general chat.

"Having Bea is a way of starting a conversation. Once the initial introductions have been made, it is easier to chat about all sorts of things, while the patients relax and pet the dog. For the last few weeks I have been talking to some old ladies who used to live in Wandsworth where I work; they have been telling me about what it was like when they lived there, and I have been describing the way it is now. There

Bea bringing comfort to elderly hospital patients.

are also a few retired police officers, now in their seventies or eighties, and we have been sharing experiences.

"For Bea, visiting is enjoyable not only because she gets lots of attention from others, but she is able to spend time alone with me. She isn't jealous of my other dogs (a Springer Spaniel, a Longhaired Dachshund, a Border Collie, and a German Shepherd)—they all get on very well—but she wants to be with me as much as she can.

"In the early days Bea was taught to track, which is to follow a human scent on all different types of terrain, and to find lost or stolen property such as keys, wallets and articles from incidents and scenes of crimes. I think Bea would have made a very good police dog.

"Ellie, my German Shepherd police dog, is lovely, but the Labrador is my breed of choice. Labs are not too demanding, but they are very loyal. They have lovely temperaments, and this makes them so popular as therapy dogs. Bea would be missed greatly if she stopped visiting.

"Bea always has a smile for you in everything she does, and sometimes she 'talks' as if she understands everything that is going on. With her shining dark eyes and the wag of her tail she makes a loyal and trustworthy friend."

THERAPY DOGS

Therapy dogs don't do a full-time job, as the other assistance dogs do, but they still help to improve people's lives. Therapy dogs visit people of all ages who are unable to have a dog of their own—whether in hospitals, hospices, schools, residential homes, or prisons.

Numerous studies have shown that stroking an animal is beneficial to people's health and well-being. This is especially important for dedicated pet owners who may have had pets throughout their lives, and are suddenly deprived of contact with animals.

The benefits of the visits can often be seen long after the dog has gone home. The visits add variety to what can sometimes be a monotonous, routine day, and can be a talking point for people, who may then go on to chat about different pets they have owned.

In schools, therapy dogs do a great job in educating children about dogs—especially those who have never had them as pets and who may fear them. Showing that dogs can be fun, loving companions helps to promote the future of our pets.

With his sociable nature, and love of being loved, it is no surprise that the Labrador is the most popular therapy dog. Having a cuddle with a waggy, smiley Lab is guaranteed to lift most people's spirits, whatever their age or circumstances.

CHAPTER SEVEN

SEEKING PERFECTION

Each and every feature of the Labrador Retriever is there for a good reason. The conformation and the temperament that identifies the breed was developed entirely because, at the beginning of the 19th century, country gentlemen wanted a dog that would be a pleasant companion around the home and a steady assistant in the shooting field. Breeding only from the very best stock, those early pioneers are responsible for giving us the modern Labrador—a wonderful breed that is known and loved throughout the world.

The characteristics of the Labrador, both physical and mental, are described in the Breed Standard, a document that gives a word picture of the real essence of the ideal Labrador—exactly how he should look and behave.

When the Standard was first drawn up by the Labrador Retriever Club in 1916, it was designed with a working dog in mind. In those days, all Labradors were primarily gundogs and only a few of them were shown.

The present British and American Standards are based on the original 1916 Standard, and only minor changes have been made over the years, so the working chacteristics of the breed still feature prominently. Here follows a summary of the two Standards.

BREED STANDARD

General Appearance

The Labrador Breed Standard describes a strongly built, well-balanced, very active dog, strong in loin and hindquarters.

Characteristics

The Labrador should be good-tempered, very agile, with an excellent nose, soft mouth, and love of water. Adaptable and loving, he should make a devoted companion.

Temperament

He should be intelligent, sharp, and biddable, with a strong will to please. He should be neither aggressive nor shy.

Head and Skull

The skull should be broad, with a defined stop creating the impression of a pronounced brow. The powerful jaws should be of medium length (ideally the same length as the skull), and should not be at all "snipy" (long, thin, and pointed). The length of the muzzle is important, bearing in mind that the dog should be able to pick up and carry heavy game in the shooting field.

The cheeks should be clean-cut, not fleshy or excessively muscled, as these qualities might cause the dog to damage its game by grasping too firmly.

The nose should be wide, and the nostrils should be well developed. This allows the dog to breathe easily while carrying game. No reference to nose color is given in the British Standard, but the American Standard states that black or yellow dogs should have black noses, and the chocolates should be brown-nosed.

Ears

The ears, which should be set quite far back, should not be large or heavy, and should hang quite close to the head.

Eyes

The medium-sized eyes should be very expressive, showing the breed's intelligence and good temper. The British Breed Standard states

The Labrador's eyes are very expressive, showing intelligence and good temper.

that brown or hazel eyes are acceptable; the American Standard is more specific, saying that black Labradors should have brown eyes, with hazel being the preferred color for yellow and chocolate Labradors. Eye rims should be pigmented.

Mouth

The jaws and teeth should be strong, and a regular scissor-bite is required (meaning the upper teeth slightly overlap the lower teeth). The scissor-bite is by far the best bite for a retriever, as it enables the dog to grip its game firmly, without fear of dropping it.

Forequarters

The neck should be strong and powerful. The shoulders should be long and sloping.

The neck and shoulder placement is very important: it gives the dog the ability to take ground scent while seeking game, then to pick it up gently and carry it back to its handler. The length and strength of the neck enable it to carry heavy game, holding it high off the ground when running back to the handler. If you could visualize or feel the bone structure, you would find a long, sloping shoulder blade, which slopes down to a well-angulated upper arm (humerus bone). These joints give the dog the ability to bend his head down to the ground while on the move, and also act as shock-absorbers when the dog jumps over fences or works on rough ground.

Without this correct angulation, the dog would jar the joints and could be injured.

From the elbow to the ground, the forelegs should be straight.

Body

The body should be strong, with a wide, deep chest and a well-sprung rib cage. The dog needs good heart and lung room to enable him to work tirelessly throughout a long day in the field. The ribs need to be of good depth and length, and the loin should be neither too long nor too short. Although the Labrador is described as a "short-coupled" dog, *too* short a loin will prevent the dog from galloping freely.

Hindquarters

The hindquarters are the powerhouse that give propulsion when the Labrador is moving. The dog should have a strong backline, not sloping toward the tail, and well-developed hindquarters. He needs well-muscled thighs, with the stifle ("knee joint") and hocks being well angulated to give enough spring to jump a fence, even when carrying heavy game. This angulation also acts as the required rear shock-absorbers to help prevent injury. Cow hocks (where the hocks turn in toward each other) are undesirable, and lessen the dog's power in movement.

The body is strong, with a wide, deep chest.

Feet

The feet should be compact, with well-arched toes and well-developed pads. Many Labradors have webbed feet, which are very useful when swimming.

Tail

The tail is a distinctive feature of the breed and is known as an "otter tail," being thick at the base and tapering to the tip in a similar way to the otter's tail. It should be of medium length, covered in thick, dense coat, and should not curl over the back.

The tail is a vital part of the Labrador's equipment; it acts as a counterbalance and braking device when the dog is on the move or changing direction. It is a rudder in the water, and is the essential Labrador signal of happiness. Labradors the world over continuously wag their tails, whether they are family pets going for a walk, show dogs performing in the ring, gundogs merrily working in the shooting field, or assistance dogs helping their owners.

Gait/Movement

The movement should be effortless, remaining straight, true, and purposeful, with the dog using his strength and power to cover the ground freely.

Coat

Originally required to work in icy waters in Newfoundland, the Labrador developed a coat that could deal with these harsh conditions. Labradors have a dense, double coat, consisting of a waterproof topcoat, which feels hard to the touch and which repels water. This, together with the thick, warm undercoat, protects the dog, not only in icy water, but also in dense woodland or thick cover.

There should be no waving or feathering of the coat.

Color

There are three Labrador coat colors—wholly black, yellow, or chocolate (liver). The yellow color covers all shades from pale cream to fox red. The coat should be of solid color, although in yellows there is often slight shading over the "saddle" area and underparts. Occasionally, in all three colors, there might be a small white spot on the chest. This is permissible, although in show ring terms is not desirable.

The three Labrador colors: chocolate, black, and yellow.

Size

British Labradors are slightly smaller than their American cousins. The ideal height for dogs, as stated in the KC Breed Standard is 56–57 cm (22–22.5 in.) and, for bitches, 54–56 cm (21.5–22 in.). The AKC states 22.5–24.5 in. (57–62 cm) for dogs, and 21.5–23.5 in. (54.5–59.5 cm) for bitches. A weight of 65–80 lb. (29.5–36 kg) for dogs, and 55–70 lb. (25–31 kg) for bitches is also given as an approximate weight of Labradors in good, working condition. No weight is given in the British Standard.

BREEDING CHAMPIONS

Breeding should never be purely for sentimental reasons. Many people let their bitch mate the dog next door because they want a "souvenir" of a well-loved pet. This kind of breeding ruins the breed. Breeding should only be done to improve the breed. Only the very best examples of the breed should be used.

However, breeding a successful show bitch to an equally successful dog is no guarantee of producing a good healthy litter of pups. Matching dogs to suitable mates is an art. Considerable research should be done into the dogs' pedigrees, looking into any recurrent health problems in the lines, the dogs' temperaments, and the physical type that is produced. The breeder should look to compensate one dog's area of weakness with another dog's strengths.

Needless to say, breeding is best left to those with years of experience. There are thousands of wonderful Labradors of all ages in rescue centers, just waiting for a good home. If you want another Lab, consider one of these, instead of contributing to the rescue crisis by breeding a litter so you can have one pup, and then not being able to find good homes for the other eight or so.

UNDERSTANDING PEDIGREES

When you bought your Labrador puppy, you may have been given some pedigree papers. Although they may look rather incomprehensible at first, it is worth spending some time reading them properly, as they give a fascinating insight into the breeding that went into producing your special pup.

There are three types of breeding: in-breeding (where closely related dogs are bred together); line-breeding (where more distantly related dogs are used); and out-crossing, where totally unrelated dogs are mated.

Given the health problems that the Labrador can be prone to, in-breeding is very rarely used. Breeding two very closely related animals (e.g., father to daughter, brother to sister) not only enhances the qualities they share genetically, it can also worsen any faults, bequeathing possible eye and hip trouble to any future generations.

The two following pedigrees illustrate how line-breeding and out-crossing can both produce Show Champions.

Line-Breeding

Sandylands, which specializes in line-breeding, is a very influential kennel, and has been for a number of years. One of the kennel's greatest dogs, Ch. Sandyland's Mark (born July 1965), sired 29 British Champions (from different dams), which to this day is still a breed record. Some of his offspring were exported and became Champions in their own countries.

Almost 30 years and five generations later, the kennel has produced Sh. Ch. Sandylands Gad-About (born November 1994), who is line-bred to Sandylands Bramble (a very influential brood bitch). He has gained the Top Labrador Sire (*Our Dogs*) prize for two consecutive years, and has produced Champions in Britain and other countries.

Line-breeding: Sh. Ch. Sandylands Gad-About.

Parents	Grandparents	Great-grandparents	Great-great-grandparents
Ch. Sandylands My Guy	Ch. Kupros Master Mariner	Sh. Ch. Lindall Mastercraft	Ch. Charway Ballywill Will
			Morningtown Stormette
		Kupros Bridget	Ch. Ballyduff Marketeer
			Ch. Kupros Lady's Pride
	Sandylands Bramble	Ch. Squire Of Ballyduff	Ch. Ballyduff Marketeer
			Sparkle Of Tuddenham
		Sh. Ch. Sandylands Longley Come Rain	Sandylands Charlston
			Longley In Tune
Sh. Ch. Sandylands Bliss	Ch. Trenow Brigadier	Joline Inkling Of Follytower	Sh. Ch. Astonbrook Crusader
			Follytower Storming Lass
		Trenow Minuet	Secret Song Of Lawnwood
			Roseacre Madonna Of Trenow
	Sandylands Rae	Sh. Ch. Ransom Of Sandylands	Sh. Ch. Sandylands My Rainbeau
			Bonfield Lady
		Sandylands Bramble	Ch. Squire Of Ballyduff
			Sh. Ch. Sandylands Longley Come Rain

Out-Crossing

All That Jazz is mostly an out-cross with nothing in common on either side of the pedigree for four generations. Breeders Joyce and Leslie Brabban believe it is their strong bitch line that helped produce such good out-cross Show Champions.

"We had a good sound bitch line, which was dominant, having few faults and lots of substance," says Joyce. "These qualities are so important in a brood bitch, especially when breeding to an out-cross.

"All That Jazz was out-crossed a few times and produced four British Champions and four foreign Champions. One very successful outcross was when we used the yellow dog Sh. Ch. Rocheby Royal Oak. This mating produced a Belgian and International Ch. Cambremer Royal Magician, also the U.S. Champions Cambremer Tudor Minstrel and Cambremer Funny Girl."

Out-cross breeding: Sh. Ch. Cambremer All That Jazz.

Ch. Kupros Master Mariner (B)	Sh. Ch./US Ch. Lindall Mastercraft (B)	Ch. Charway Ballywill Will (B)	Ballyduff Spruce (B)
			Charway Simona (B)
		Morningtown Stormette (C)	Ch. Follytower Merrybrook Black Stormer (B)
			Morningtown Toblar (C)
	Kupros Bridget (B)	Ch. Ballyduff Marketeer (B)	Ch. Sandylands Mark (B)
			Ch. Ballyduff Marina (B)
		Ch. Kupros Lady's Pride (B)	Ch. Squire Of Ballyduff (B)
			Kupros My Lady (B)
Cambremer Montclair (B)	Ch. Fabracken Comedy Star (B)	Sh. Ch. Martin Of Mardas (B)	Ch. Ballyduff Marketeer (B)
			Mardas Vivette (B)
		Ch. Poolstead Pin Up Of Fabracken (B)	Ch. Sandylands Mark (B)
			Poolstead Pincushion (Y)
	Sh. Ch. Cambremer St. Clair (Y)	Sh. Ch. Glenarem Skyrocket (Y)	Glenarem Consort (Y)
			Sh. Ch. Glenarem Caprice (Y)
		Braunspath Simona Of Cambremer (Y)	Sh. Ch. Longley Count On (Y)
			Pollyester Of Sixhills (Y)

PUPPY TO CHAMPION

Ch. Fabracken Comedy Star ('Murphy')

Murphy at five weeks.

Four months of age.

Ch. Fabracken Comedy Star.

This series of photos shows the development of Ch. Fabracken Comedy Star from five weeks through to 11 years. As you can see, the Labrador not only grows in height, but also in head, body and coat, as well.

Ch. Fabracken Comedy Star (born 1979) held 36 CCs and 24 Reserve CCs, making him the top-winning black Labrador in the U.K. As well as being a top winner in the show ring and siring Champions in different countries around the world, he also held a working certificate, and sired several Field Trial and Working Test award winners.

CHAPTER EIGHT

HEALTH CARE

Trevor Turner BVetMed, MRCVS

The Labrador Retriever is a sporting dog and part of the gundog group as far as the British Kennel Club is concerned, while the American Kennel Club, with its slightly different grouping system, classifies it in Group 1: Sporting Dogs, where it is listed as "Retriever, Labrador."

Due to temperament and general disposition, the Labrador is one of the most popular dogs in the world. In 1998 nearly 36,000 were registered in Britain alone, with nearly 158,000 in the United States, and registrations only represent a small proportion of the total number of puppies bred each year.

In this context it is hardly surprising that the Labrador does have a number of problems associated with the breed, but this, compared with some other breeds, is remarkably small.

Like all working dogs, they are active, energetic animals and, as such, have suffered their fair share of joint and bone problems, hip dysplasia being one of the most common. However, due to eradication programs actively pursued by breed clubs, this disabling disease is now much less widespread than a few years ago.

Hereditary eye disease is also subject to a similar control program and thus, when contemplating the purchase of a Labrador puppy, it is recommended that you inquire from the breeders the status of the parents in respect of these problems.

PREVENTIVE CARE

Mention preventive care to most dog owners and vaccination immediately springs to mind. However, there is more to it than that. Labradors are working dogs, but nevertheless make excellent pets. Their temperaments are such that they are everybody's friend.

In exchange for this unrivalled temperament, we have to give something in return. They should not be turned into indolent toys. Too often one hears the term "fat Labrador" and, in

view of their history and track record, fat they should not be, and it is in our hands as responsible owners to ensure obesity does not occur. Thus preventive care involves a correctly balanced diet and regular exercise, as well as routine attention to parasite control. The owner must deal both with parasites on the outside (ectoparasites), such as fleas, ticks, and lice, and those on the inside (endoparasites), such as roundworms, tapeworms, and hookworms, together with heartworms, which are significant in parts of the U.S. and southern Europe.

Vaccination

Dogs, like people, can develop a natural immunity as the result of exposure to disease. For example, infectious bronchitis, or tracheitis, **kennel cough**, is extremely contagious. When in contact with the organism *Bordetella bronchiseptica*, uninoculated dogs, without any immunity, can pick up the bacteria, develop signs (such as coughing—sometimes for up to three weeks), recover, and then have good immunity for six months or so.

So it was in the days when distemper was rife. Distemper was considerably more serious a disease in the days before vaccination. A lot of dogs died, but those that survived had a solid immunity that was continuously reinforced—because every time they went out and came in contact with other dogs, they were likely to be challenged by the virus, since it was so prevalent.

Passive immunity fades soon after a puppy has been weaned.

However, as with all the killer diseases, more dogs succumbed than recovered and became immune, and it was for this reason that vaccines were developed.

Vaccination (inoculation) stimulates the dog to produce active immunity against one, or a collection of, diseases without developing signs of that disease. The puppy acquires its first immunity from the dam while in the womb. This is delivered via the bloodstream across the placenta. After birth, that immunity is boosted while suckling. This is **passive immunity** and, once the puppy is weaned, it soon fades. It is at this time that the puppy should receive primary vaccination to stimulate its own immunity, which will protect it just as natural immunity protected the dog that survived the natural disease.

Today, due to vaccination, many of the serious killer diseases are no longer rife, and, therefore, natural challenge does not occur. The immunity acquired from the primary vaccination does not last and so regular boosters are advised.

Inoculation and vaccination are used synonymously throughout the chapter. Strictly, inoculation means introducing the agent into the tissues of the body to stimulate an immune response. It usually involves an injection, but the human smallpox vaccine, for example, used to be inoculated by scarifying the skin of the arm.

Vaccination similarly stimulates the subject to produce immunity against a disease without developing signs, but need not necessarily be directly introduced into the tissues of the body. Thus, vaccination against infectious tracheitis (kennel cough) using Bordetella vaccine is achieved by instilling a few drops up the nose.

Primary vaccination should be started as soon as the passively acquired immunity from the bitch has declined sufficiently to allow the puppy to develop its own active immunity.

Immunity Gap

The so-called immunity gap has always been the problem with canine vaccinations. In order that the vaccine can stimulate the puppy's immunity, circulating maternal antibodies must have fallen sufficiently. Vaccination takes time to stimulate the puppy's active immunity and during this period the puppy is vulnerable to infection. This occurs at the same time as the owner's necessary efforts to ensure that the puppy meets as many new experiences as possible, in order to mature into a well-integrated family dog.

Today we have vaccines that have been shown to give a workable immunity at ten weeks of age, which ensures that these puppies do not have to be virtually isolated until approximately four months of age, as once was the case.

As soon as you have acquired your new puppy, call your local veterinarian and inquire about the practice's vaccination policy. Also, discuss appointment details, price, etc., and whether the practice organizes puppy classes or knows where these are available. These are extremely valuable in the case of the Labrador, since they are tremendous extroverts and controlled introduction to fresh faces, be they dogs or people, from an early age is all part of the training process, ensuring that you ultimately achieve a well-trained, well-mannered Labrador.

"Ask your vet for advice about a suitable vaccination program"

Boosters

Following primary vaccination, revaccination (boosters) will be necessary from time to time. Veterinarians on both sides of the Atlantic cannot, at the present time, state authoritatively how often these should be administered. Originally, it was advised that we should revaccinate against all the diseases each year. This still makes economic sense, since multivalent vaccines (those containing components against several diseases) cost less overall than vaccination against each individual disease.

Ask your veterinarian for advice about boosters.

However, there has been recent concern that some dogs develop adverse reactions to multivalent boosters. This has led to a re-examination of the necessity for the annual shot, particularly since there is evidence that inoculation (vaccination) against certain diseases can last longer than one year.

My personal view is that the risk of reaction is so slight, compared with the threat of disease in the unprotected dog, that I still tend to go for annual boosters every time. This is based on more than 40 years of clinical experience, during which I encountered distemper, hepatitis, and, in the 1980s, parvovirus in epidemic proportions. Despite intensive treatment, I lost many dogs with these serious conditions but I have never had to treat a dog with a serious vaccine reaction.

If in doubt, discuss the matter carefully with your veterinarian. The time of the primary vaccination is a good opportunity. However, whatever you do, do not omit to have that first protective vaccination course administered, since it is the puppy that is at greatest risk once maternal immunity has waned.

Can We Measure Immunity?

Blood tests are available for both puppies and adult dogs, and will indicate the level of immune response for any of the diseases that we vaccinate against. These give a guide to revaccination. Blood testing can be expensive since the blood test for each disease will probably cost as much as the combined booster against all the diseases. Cost apart, is this procedure better for the pets?

Blood sampling is, without doubt, stressful for the puppy—even if that means only that the exuberant baby Labrador has to be held still while it is being done. With the older Labrador, it very much depends on his previous veterinary experiences; the majority will no doubt take it in their stride. Nevertheless, I am sure that, if we could canvass their opinion, they would much prefer the simple booster vaccination, which involves a subcutaneous (under the skin) injection, done in a flash!

Some vaccines do not endow a long-lasting immunity. *Bordetella bronchiseptica* vaccine against infectious tracheitis (kennel cough), involving nasal drops, only lasts approximately eight months; so, if you board your dog regularly or attend training classes, shows, competitions, etc., revaccination against infectious tracheitis every six months should be seriously considered.

Kennel cough has low mortality but high morbidity. In other words, it does not often prove fatal, but the dog may cough for several weeks, and, even when apparently recovered, may still be infectious. Vaccination, although it may not be 100 percent effective, at least alleviates the worry.

Kennel cough spreads quickly among a resident population of dogs.

The other components of kennel cough are viruses—adenovirus (hepatitis), distemper virus, and parainfluenza virus. These are all incorporated in multivalent (multi-disease) vaccines. They should all give a workable immunity for at least a year and some even longer.

"The signs of hepatitis can vary widely in severity"

Leptospira vaccines are also usually included in the primary multivalent vaccination course. These are killed bacterial vaccines and only provide a workable immunity in the average dog for about 12 months.

Modified live virus vaccines, such as those used to give protection against distemper or hepatitis, give a much longer period of protection, but this again varies with the individual. However, recent work has shown that it is considerably longer than one year.

Due to the efficacy of multivalent vaccines and the lack of concrete evidence in respect of the adverse effects of boosting, little work has been done to establish exactly how necessary revaccination is, or how often it should be carried out. My view is that it is better to be safe than sorry and since I personally have no concrete evidence that boosting, even if not entirely necessary, does any harm, I prefer to be safe rather than sorry.

If you have any anxieties regarding booster vaccination, take time to discuss the matter with your veterinarian.

Core and Non-Core Vaccines

Because of the concern of dog owners regarding the possible adverse effects associated with vaccination or overvaccination, there is a move in the United States to divide vaccinations into two groups: Core Vaccines and Non-Core Vaccines.

Core Vaccines are the necessary ones that protect against the disease that is serious, fatal, or difficult to treat. In the U.K., these include distemper, parvovirus, and hepatitis (adenovirus). In North America, rabies is also included. This is likely to occur in the U.K. in the not-too-distant future, as a result of the change in quarantine regulations.

Non-Core Vaccines include Bordetella, leptospirosis, coronavirus, and borrelia (Lyme disease) since it is known that this latter vaccine can cause reactions in a number of dogs.

PREVENTABLE CONDITIONS

Distemper

Solely due to vaccination, canine distemper is no longer widespread. Signs (symptoms) include fever, diarrhea, coughing, and discharges from the nose and eyes. Sometimes the pads harden so that, when walking over a hard floor, the poor dog will sound like a pony. This is the so-called hardpad variant. A high proportion of infected dogs develop nervous signs, fits, chorea (twitching of muscle groups), and paralysis. Distemper virus can also sometimes be involved in infectious tracheitis.

Hepatitis

Hepatitis (adenovirus disease) is another killer disease of dogs that has been successfully combated with vaccination. Signs can vary from sudden death, to mild cases where the dog is just a bit "off-color." In severe cases, there is usually fever, enlargement of all the lymph nodes (glands), and a swollen liver. During recovery the dog can develop a "blue eye" and may look blind. This is due to edema (swelling) of the cornea, which is the clear part in front of the eye. Although initially worrying, this usually resolves without lasting effects. Adenovirus is also one of the components in infectious tracheitis, the kennel cough syndrome.

Parainfluenza

Multivalent vaccines on both sides of the Atlantic usually include a parainfluenza component. Parainfluenza virus is considered to be the main cause of infectious tracheitis in North America, whereas, in the U.K., the bacterium *Bordetella bronchiseptica* is considered to be the primary cause.

Rabies

Rabies vaccination is mandatory in many countries, including the U.S., and, with relaxation of quarantine regulations, may well become so in the U.K. It is an extremely serious disease, not only because, like all virus diseases, it is untreatable, but also because it is communicable to humans (zoonotic). Modern vaccines are extremely effective in preventing the disease.

Rabies vaccination is mandatory in many countries.

It should be remembered that all the virus diseases, even those such as parainfluenza, which have a relatively low mortality rate, are not susceptible to antibiotics; treatment is merely supportive of the patient, hoping that the dog's immunity will fight and overcome the virus (and at the same time build up an immune response!). Bacterial diseases, on the other hand, are treatable with antibiotics, but, depending on the disease, vaccination is sometimes preferable.

Bordetellosis

It is also called infectious tracheitis, infectious bronchitis, or kennel cough. It causes a persistent cough, and is not usually life-threatening, except in young puppies and elderly dogs.

In the U.K., the bacterium *Bordetella bronchiseptica* is the usual primary cause, although viruses can be secondarily implicated. These include distemper, hepatitis, and parainfluenza virus. In the U.S., it is this latter virus that is considered the main cause, with Bordetella a secondary invader.

The Bordetella component is not included in the multivalent vaccine because it is usually administered as nasal drops, a route of administration that gives rapid and effective protection.

Leptospirosis

There are many different bacteria of the leptospira group, but two are incorporated into leptospirosis vaccines for dogs. Both infections are important because they regularly kill affected dogs and they can cause serious human disease.

Leptospira icterohaemorrhagiae is mainly an infection of rats, but affects dogs, as well as people (Weil's disease), and other animals. *Leptospiral canicola* is mainly a canine infection, but can also affect man. The main source of infection is the urine of infected animals—rat urine in the case of *L. icterohaemorrhagiae*, whereas *L. canicola* is spread mainly in urban areas from a reservoir of unvaccinated dogs.

Both diseases can cause serious liver conditions and, especially with *L. canicola*, recovered dogs can shed the bacteria in their urine for several months.

The bacterial reservoir of these carrier dogs lies in the kidney and the body's attempt to destroy these bacteria can sometimes result in serious reduction of kidney function and thus the dog dies of kidney failure.

"The Lab's love of water can make him susceptible to leptospirosis"

With *L. icterohaemorrhagiae*, severe liver dysfunction occurs that results in swelling of the liver and severe dehydration and shock, which can result in death. There is usually black diarrhea, the dog becomes jaundiced, and may develop blood patches on the skin and in the lining of the mouth and eyes. With *L. canicola* there is initially a similar phase of dullness and loss of appetite, but kidney failure can occur a week or two later.

Vaccines against both types of leptospirae are combined as part of the standard puppy vaccination program. They are killed inactivated vaccines and two doses are required to give approximately one year's immunity. Many countries require that imported dogs be free from evidence of leptospiral infection.

Leptospira vaccination should always be carefully considered in the case of the Labrador, as his well-known liking for water makes him particularly susceptible to infection, especially in areas where rats are rife.

Lyme Disease

This is caused by a bacterium that is transmitted through the bite of ticks that causes an inflammatory disease in many species, including dogs and man. Clinical diagnosis is difficult because signs can vary. Most commonly, there are arthritis-like conditions accompanied by fever. Cardiac, kidney, and neurological problems can also occur.

It is relatively rare in the U.K., although very common in certain parts of America, where the difficulty of positive diagnosis makes prevention via vaccination well worthwhile.

Exercise Needs

Labradors are extremely active dogs and they do require regular exercise. They are intelligent and eager to please, and, in skilled hands, are relatively easy to train. Once you are confident of their recall abilities, there is nothing they enjoy more than a free ramble in suitable open space and this, to them, is more important than the weather. With their thick, protective double-coat, a hike through an icy December gale is just as enjoyable as a midsummer saunter along a woodland path. Be prepared! This is part of your ongoing commitment and, with luck, may remain so for ten years or so. Labradors are extremely energetic and do need that exercise. Off the lead, in the time it takes you to walk a couple of miles, they will probably have covered over ten miles and still be ready for more.

Obesity

Fat, aging Labradors are not an uncommon sight. A small percentage are not "owner mistakes." Despite the owner doing all the right things, the dog has still become obese with age. However, the majority of overweight Labradors undoubtedly owe their condition to their

Regular exercise is a must for healthy Labradors.

The breeder's aim is to create a line of sound, typical dogs.

owners. Like all gundogs, Labradors are not fastidious eaters and an injudicious diet with too many food treats, too much fat, and too much carbohydrate will soon result in an overweight dog that is then less inclined to exercise.

Food rewards are splendid training aids for the breed, but do not overdo it. If you have any concerns regarding the weight of your Labrador, consult your veterinarian without delay. Today, there are excellent diets that will correct the problem before it becomes irreversible.

Parasites

Control of parasites is also part of preventive health care. Labradors are, at heart, outdoor dogs, so it is not surprising that parasites can be a problem without preventive care. These include **ectoparasites**, such as fleas, lice, ticks, and mites, and **endoparasites**, of which worms (both roundworms and tapeworms) are the main challenge.

Fleas

Fleas are the most common ectoparasites found on dogs worldwide. Some Labradors can carry high flea burdens with few signs and often, because of their thick, dense coat, the fleas go unseen by the owners. On the other hand, some Labradors will develop a flea-allergy dermatitis as the result of only a few flea bites. The hypersensitivity of these unfortunate individuals is due to the injection of flea saliva when the dog it bitten, and it is to this that the dog is allergic. This causes intense irritation and the dog starts to mutilate himself as a result. These are the dogs that require very vigilant flea control.

Unfortunately, owners are frequently unconvinced that fleas are the main problem, since, despite diligent searching, sometimes no fleas can be found in the coat. However, there is usually evidence of tell-tale flea dirt, which looks like tiny pieces of black grit.

Fleas are not host-specific. Both dog and cat fleas can be found on dogs, cats, and humans. Raccoons can also be a major source of fleas in parts of North America. Irrespective of the original host, all types can bite a variety of animals, including man.

The eggs and larval form of the flea develop off the host. Development depends upon humidity and temperature. In warm environments, the life cycle is completed in days rather than weeks and it is for this reason that fleas are such a problem in the northern states in summertime and in the southern states of the U.S. all the year round.

Effective flea control involves eradication of adult fleas on the dog (even if you haven't actually seen any!) and also the immature stages that develop in the environment. Obviously, control of developing fleas in the yard is not practicable, particularly if continuously reinfested from visiting animals.

Fleas need a meal of blood to complete their life cycle. They feed on the dog and then lay eggs, which develop in the environment. Development of the next generation, depending on temperature and humidity, can be as short as three weeks. Fleas can also survive in suitable environments for more than a year without feeding. This is the reason why dogs—and people—can be bitten when entering properties left unoccupied.

Flea Control

Preventive measures in the home should include thorough vacuuming to remove immature stages. The use of an environmental insecticide, with prolonged action to kill any developing fleas, must also be considered since few insecticides currently on the market kill flea larvae.

Treatment of your dog can be with oral medication, which prevents completion of the flea life cycle, or the use of sprays, powders, or spot preparations to kill any adult fleas present. Insecticidal baths effectively kill adult fleas in the coat but do not have any residual effect; therefore bathing, although immediately effective, must be combined with other methods of flea control.

Modern spot preparations will give reasonable protection lasting up to two months or even longer, and these are still effective even if your dog is bathed several times in between applications. The insecticide spreads through the invisible fat layer covering the skin without

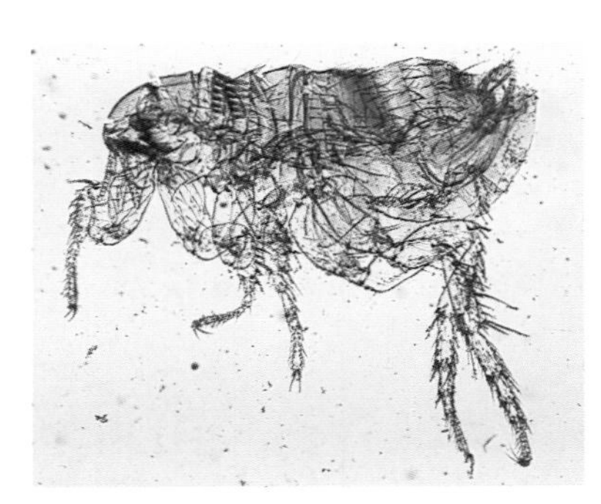

The dog flea—(Ctenocephalides canis)

actually getting into the body, thus within 24 hours the dog will have total protection against fleas. When a flea bites the dog it has to penetrate this fat layer and thus ingest the chemical, but the product has not actually entered the dog's body. These preparations are very safe, but, occasionally, sensitive Labradors will show an allergic reaction at the point of application, which is usually on the neck where the dog cannot lick at it.

Other preparations are available in the form of powders, sprays, and collars.

If you are unfortunate enough to have a Labrador that has a flea-allergy dermatitis, you must use something to kill the adult fleas and so prevent your dog from being bitten and from flea saliva being injected, which causes the allergic itching.

Oral medication preventing the completion of the life cycle is effective for long-term control, but does nothing to kill the mature fleas that are causing the irritation misery by biting the hypersensitive pet for that all-essential blood meal.

Dogs that live in the country are more likely to pick up ticks.

Lice

Lice are not as common as fleas, and are usually seen in puppies or young dogs that have been reared in perhaps less than ideal conditions. They usually require direct contact for transmission and the whole life cycle occurs on the host. The eggs (nits) are attached to individual hairs and can be seen with the naked eye.

Infestation is invariably associated with violent irritation. Bathing in insecticidal shampoos, such as those suitable for fleas, is usually effective.

Ticks

These can be a problem in certain areas. In the English suburbs, they are frequently carried on hedgehogs. In rural areas, sheep are usually the primary host. In North America, certain ticks are carriers of Lyme disease.

As for fleas and lice, there is a variety of insecticidal products available. Some spray and spot preparations have prolonged activity even if the dog is bathed between applications. They do not prevent the tick from attaching, but it will soon die.

Harvest Mites

These are bright orange/red larval mites that are just visible to the naked eye. They are particularly prevalent in areas with chalky soil, especially around harvest time.

They are the larvae of a mite that is not parasitic (i.e., is free-living) and lives in decaying organic matter. They cause intense irritation and dermatitis, particularly around the feet and muzzle.

Prolonged-action insecticidal sprays are recommended since reinfestation is likely, particularly in autumn.

"Heavy worm infestation can be fatal to small puppies"

Mange

Mange is a parasitic skin disease caused by microscopic mites, two of which can affect dogs.

Demodectic Mange

The demodectic mite lives in the hair follicles, and, as long as the dog's immune system is functioning, these mites cause little harm. However, if your Labrador does have an immune system problem, the demodectic mites can undergo a population explosion and cause hair loss in patches, particularly on the face and around the eyes. Since it is only a problem in the immuno-incompetent dog, it is not particularly contagious, but, due to secondary infection, can create major problems for the dog.

Sarcoptic Mange

In the U.K. and parts of Europe, sarcoptic mange is spread mainly by foxes, and is highly contagious not only to other dogs but also to humans, particularly children. Labradors, with their outdoor lifestyle, can be particularly prone, especially puppies and young dogs.

Diagnosis of both types of mange depends on identification of the causal mite under a microscope. Various applications and shampoos are available for treatment, but these should only be used as advised by your veterinarian.

Endoparasites

For your Labrador, worms are by far the most important endoparasites, but do remember there are others. *Coccidia* and *Giardia*, which are tiny one-celled organisms, can sometimes cause problems associated with chronic diarrhea and lack of growth in puppies.

Roundworms and tapeworms are the most important endoparasites in respect of routine preventive care.

Roundworms

Nematodes, or roundworms, especially the *Toxocara* species, are the most common worms found in the dog. Because of their complicated life cycle and the fact that puppies can be born with worms acquired from their mother before birth, roundworms are virtually ubiquitous in puppies.

The most common roundworm is *Toxocara canis*. It is a large white roundworm, 3–6 in.

(7–15 cm) long. There are many effective worm treatments, but few work against larval (juvenile) stages. Roundworm larvae remain dormant in the tissue of adult dogs but, in the bitch, under the influence of the hormones of pregnancy, they become activated, cross the placenta and enter the puppy where they finally develop into adult worms in the small intestine. Thus Labrador puppies can be passing *Toxocara* eggs as early as eleven days after birth. The larvae are also passed from the bitch to the puppy in the milk and via the feces.

Adult dogs should be wormed routinely about twice a year, since there is a slight risk that humans can become infected with roundworms from dogs, and children can be particularly vulnerable.

Puppies with larvae developing rapidly within their bodies should be wormed from approximately two weeks of age. Treatment should be repeated regularly until the puppy is at least six months old.

Effective preparations are on sale in supermarkets and pet stores, but it is nevertheless worthwhile discussing an effective worming strategy with your veterinarian.

In the puppy, a heavy infestation causes many problems, from generalized ill health to diarrhea and vomiting, obstruction of the bowel, and even death. Adult dogs can carry heavy worm burdens if not regularly wormed, but show surprisingly few signs.

Tapeworms

Cestodes, or tapeworms, are the other major class of worm found in the dog. Unlike roundworms, they have an indirect life cycle so do not spread directly from dog to dog. Intermediate hosts vary from fleas to sheep or horses, depending on the type of tapeworm. The most common tapeworm in the dog is *Dipylidium caninum*. Fleas are the intermediate host. Flea larvae developing in the environment swallow the microscopic tapeworm eggs shed by the dog in the feces. These mature as the flea develops. The dog consumes the flea and so the life cycle is completed.

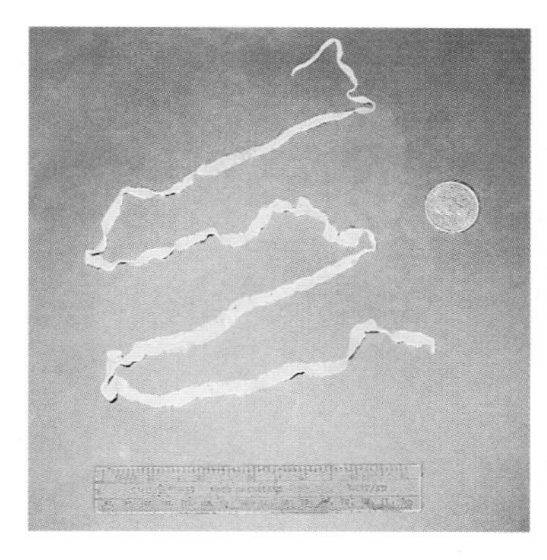

Tapeworm passed by an adult dog. (The coin gives an indication of size).

Dipylidium is a large worm and can measure up to 20 in. (50 cm). Individual segments that are passed in the feces resemble small rice grains and often stick around the dog's anus. Initially they can be seen moving. These are the recently shed moving segments containing the eggs that have to be eaten by the intermediate host to complete the life cycle.

Some effective remedies are available without prescription but it is important that fleas are also controlled, so discuss an appropriate strategy with your veterinarian.

Other species of tapeworm have intermediate hosts that include sheep, horses, rodents, and

The responsible owner should be able to follow basic first-aid procedures.

even man. There is little danger to the dog, provided raw flesh of the infested intermediate host is not fed or scavenged.

With gundogs, such as the Labrador, this is particularly important since they are quite partial to the odd rabbit or rat carcass!

Other Worms

Hookworms and whipworms are other types of worms that can affect the bowel. These are generally only a problem in kennel dogs that have grass runs. Modern multi-wormers are effective.

Canine lungworm (*Filaroides osleri*) can sometimes be responsible for intractable coughing in young Labradors. The worms live in nodules in the air passages, resulting in coughing and loss of condition. Effective veterinary treatment is available.

Heartworm caused by the roundworm (*Dirofilaria immitis*) is a major problem in many warmer parts of the world and does occur in Great Britain in some imported animals. Transmission is by bites from mosquitoes and very effective remedies are available today.

EMERGENCY CARE AND FIRST AID

Labradors are enthusiastic, exuberant dogs and can get themselves into situations that rapidly develop into emergencies. For example, in practice, I always had the impression that

Labradors seemed to suffer more cut feet than other breeds! Injuries can also result from traffic accidents, bites, fight wounds, and insect stings, as well as emergencies as a result of heat stroke, poisoning, seizures, and shock.

Injuries to the throat caused by catching sticks end-on that are thrown in play; torn claws; and bones and other objects lodged in the back of the mouth or throat are all examples of conditions requiring immediate first aid.

First aid is the initial treatment given to an emergency immediately after injury, collapse, or sudden onset of illness. The purpose is to preserve life, reduce pain and discomfort, and minimize the risk of permanent disability or disfigurement. Irrespective of the emergency, there is much that can be done by simple first aid.

Priorities

1. Keep calm and do not panic.
2. Wherever possible, get help. Contact your veterinarian, explain the situation, and obtain first-aid advice if possible.
3. If there is a possible injury, try to keep the dog as still as possible. If necessary, lay the dog on his side with the head and neck gently pressed to the ground, with your arm across the neck, if necessary holding the uninjured limbs.
4. If in shock, keep him warm by putting a blanket or some clothing over him.
5. If there is the possibility of broken bones, particularly if the spine is involved, try to keep the dog as still as possible.
6. If he cannot walk, try lifting him on a blanket carried between at least two people. If the injuries involve the back end, you may be able to move the dog by grasping him firmly around the chest and letting the hindquarters hang. You are unlikely to cause further injuries this way. Many people try to move immobile dogs on boards, doors, etc., as makeshift stretchers. The dog, if not actually unconscious, may be frightened with this unusual mode of transport and injure himself further by falling off!
7. If you do not have a station wagon, carry the dog on a blanket, place him on the back seat and make sure someone travels in the back with him if at all possible.
8. Drive carefully and observe the speed limits.

Shock

Shock is a complex condition that results in a serious fall in blood pressure. Causes include blood loss due to bleeding, heart failure, acute allergy following stings, etc., and heat stroke.

First signs include rapid breathing and increased heart rate. The mucous membranes of the gums, lips, and under the eyelids are very pale. The dog may be seriously depressed. He may vomit, and the feet or ears may feel very cold.

Warmth is important. Cover with coats, blankets, or even newspaper. Keep the dog very quiet and seek immediate veterinary help, particularly if there is any hemorrhaging, which should be controlled if at all possible.

THE A, B, AND C OF FIRST AID

A—AIRWAY
B—BREATHING
C—CARDIAC FUNCTION

Airway

This is part of the so-called ABC approach to first aid, and always comes first. Make sure the airway is clear to allow oxygen to the lungs. If your Labrador has injured his throat with a stick, has vomited or collapsed, or is choking, it is important you do your best to ensure the airway is unobstructed.

It is very important that you do not put your fingers in the dog's mouth—he will be just as frightened as you are, and, if fighting for his life, may well bite in panic. Using a tie or a pair of tights, it is sometimes possible to loop material around the upper or lower fang teeth and open the mouth. If there is an obstruction that can be removed, attempt it.

In Labradors, bones often get stuck across the hard palate between the large cheek teeth (carnassial teeth). The dog frantically tries to remove the obstruction and sometimes looks as though he is having a seizure. If you can get the mouth open without danger, you can sometimes flick the piece of bone or stick out with the back of a spoon or fork, if available. If using your bare hands, take care!

If there is a lot of fluid or blood in the mouth, try to clear this using a sponge or even a piece of cloth or clothing.

Breathing

If your dog is not breathing, try gently pumping the chest. With a hand on each side of the rib cage, just behind the elbows, which are pulled slightly forward, gently squeeze the ribs over the heart.

Cardiac Function

At the same site, try to feel a heartbeat. If there is one, attempt cardiac massage. With a hand on each side of the rib cage, just behind the elbows, which should be pulled slightly forward, gently squeeze the ribs over the heart.

Bleeding

Torn nails are not uncommon. They are extremely painful and bleed profusely, as do cut pads. A tight bandage can be improvised from any reasonably clean material. A plastic bag bandaged over the paw, between the layers of bandage, will contain the blood. The main aim is to apply as much bandaging as possible and then get the dog to the veterinarian immediately.

> ***"Learning the key points of first aid is as easy as ABC"***

If a tight bandage has been applied, do not leave it on for more than 15–20 minutes. If the site cannot be bandaged, try to stem serious bleeding by applying finger or hand pressure. Get help to transport your dog to the veterinarian immediately.

Burns and Scalds

Labradors have a tendency to get under your feet, particularly in the kitchen when you are cooking. Therefore, they can get burned, particularly with hot liquids. Luckily, their thick coat often protects them from severe injury, but if there is a possibility of a burn or scald, cool the burned area with cold water as quickly as possible.

- If burns are extensive, cover with damp towels.
- If the burn is due to a caustic substance, try to dilute this using plenty of cold water.
- If your dog has licked something caustic, e.g., drain cleaner, bleach, etc., try washing out the mouth using cloths soaked in clean cold water pressed between the jaws.

Eye Injuries

These are usually the result of trauma, cats' claws, bushes, etc. If any foreign body can be seen and easily removed, do so, otherwise cover the eye with a pad soaked in cold water, or, better still, saline solution (contact lens solution) and then seek veterinary help.

Heat Stroke

Labradors are surprisingly prone to heat stroke. The most common cause is due to being left in cars with too little ventilation in warm weather. Remember, the car need not necessarily be in direct sunlight for the heat to kill your dog.

First signs of heat stroke are excessive panting with obvious distress; unconsciousness and coma can follow frighteningly quickly.

Try to reduce body temperature by bathing with copious amounts of cold water, iced if possible, and then cover the wet animal in damp towels. Take him to the veterinarian as soon as possible. If he is not able to walk, carry him on a blanket. It will need at least two people, each taking corners. If there is likely to be a delay,

Labradors tend to get underfoot—and that is when accidents can happen.

Heat stroke occurs very rapidly when a dog is left in a car with insufficient ventilation.

continue wetting him with iced water (if available) and use a fan or hair dryer, blowing *cold* air on to him, to try to reduce his temperature as soon as possible.

Fits and Seizures

Fits due to epilepsy and other causes can occur in some Labradors and these are always frightening for the onlooker. The dog should not be stimulated while in the seizure and therefore it is better not to touch him. Left alone, injury is unlikely, particularly if any movable furniture (stools, occasional tables, etc.) is taken out of his way. A dark environment speeds recovery, so try to draw the curtains, turn off the lights, etc.

Once recovered, he will be dazed and unable to see or hear properly for a short time. Take care in handling him because he may be frightened and may not recognize you. As soon as practicable, take him to your veterinarian.

If the fit lasts for more than three to four minutes, contact your veterinarian for advice.

BREED-SPECIFIC CONDITIONS

If the popularly held belief that pedigree dogs are riddled with problems were indeed true, Labrador Retrievers, with their huge popularity, should suffer more than most. The truth is the reverse. Hugely popular as both pets and working dogs, Labradors have comparatively little breed-specific disease, particularly if compared with some other popular breeds.

Labrador breed problems fall basically into three categories:

- Epilepsy
- Eye problems
- Orthopedic problems

Epilepsy

Seizures or fits can occur and sometimes may be due to liver, renal, or cardiac problems. However, idiopathic epilepsy does occur in the Labrador. This describes the situation where fits or seizures occur with no apparent abnormalities. The condition can be hereditary and the onset of epilepsy can be between six months and five years.

Convulsions can vary from mild, almost imperceptible, incoordination to full-scale seizures where the dog becomes unconscious and can go from one fit into another. Fits in bitches are more likely to occur with the onset

The Labrador has few breed-specific conditions.

of estrus (heat), and because of this and the possible hereditary implications, neutering should be considered.

Modern drug therapy will control the condition so that the majority of Labradors suffering epilepsy can lead perfectly normal lives. However, treatment is a long-term commitment, although some dogs can be gradually weaned from their anticonvulsants.

When considering buying a Labrador Retriever, it is always worth inquiring if there has been any indication of epilepsy in the line.

Eye Problems

Various hereditary eye conditions can affect the Labrador Retriever. Many countries, including the United Kingdom and the United States, have eradication programs in progress. This program may involve regular testing by specially appointed eye panellist veterinarians who examine the dog's eyes and make a report covering all the conditions that are known to be hereditary in the Labrador or are under investigation. These include **cataracts,** which can involve ultimate blindness due to the increasing opacity of the lens. It should be remembered, however, that cataracts can occur due to other causes, for example, diabetes mellitus.

"Labradors suffer more than their fair share of bone problems"

Another part of the eye that can be affected by hereditary problems in the breed is the retina. This is the light-sensitive surface at the back of the eye which, as far as the dog is concerned, is similar to the film in a camera. It transmits to the brain the images that are focused upon it by the lens.

Progressive retinal atrophy (PRA) is a term used to describe a number of inherited retinal degenerations. In the Labrador, both generalized PRA and central PRA can occur, both of which have an hereditary basis.

With generalized PRA, total blindness can be the final outcome, but night blindness (inability to see at low light levels), is usually the first sign. Cataracts are a common secondary feature of generalized PRA.

Central PRA, on the other hand, does not usually start with night blindness and it is unusual for the dog to become totally blind, although vision may be severely affected.

Retinal dysplasia (RD) is a congenital defect which, in its most mild form, involves a multiple folding of the retina, while the most severe type results in retinal detachment and blindness.

Breed clubs worldwide are aware of these problems, and, as a result of their cooperation with eye testing, the pooling of results and pedigree analysis, there is a considerably greater chance now of obtaining a Labrador puppy free from these hereditary faults than even a decade ago. Eye-testing is required annually, so ensure that your puppy's parents each have an up-to-date certificate.

Orthopedic Conditions

Because of their exuberant, active nature, Labradors do seem to suffer more than their fair share of bone problems, some of which are undoubtedly hereditary.

Osteochondritis Dissecans (OCD)

This affects growing cartilage in the joints and can result in a loose flap of cartilage in the joint, particularly in the shoulder and the elbow. It occurs typically between four and eight months of age when the dog may suddenly show signs of lameness and pain. Treatment involving medication and/or surgery is very effective.

Growing puppies are very vulnerable to joint problems.

Hip Dysplasia

This results in abnormal looseness or laxity of the hip joints. It is a multifactorial disease involving heredity, nutrition, trauma, exercise, etc. Inheritance is not simple. It is known as a polygenic condition since there is an interaction of many genes. With this genetic disposition to the disease, overexercising the puppy will result in signs (symptoms) becoming apparent much earlier. Affected dogs usually first show signs of difficulty when rising, and may be noticed taking more weight on their front legs than normal. Sometimes lameness is not apparent until arthritis sets in, which may be as early as 15–18 months but sometimes it is much later in life. Nevertheless, it is a very crippling disease to which Labradors at one time were especially prone.

Today, again as a result of eradication programs that involve radiography (X-ray) of the dog's hips in a standard position and the scoring of these X-rays by a panel of specially trained veterinary experts, the incidence of the condition has been greatly reduced. Again, if contemplating buying a Labrador puppy, ask whether the parents have been scored for hip dysplasia.

There is now a similar program available for elbow dysplasia, a similar condition resulting in laxity and, ultimately, arthritis affecting the elbow joints.

Cruciate Ligament Rupture

The stifle (knee joint) of the dog is a hinged joint. Like a door, the knee moves only in one plane—i.e., it moves backward and forward. This is unlike the hip or the shoulder, which can move in all directions.

The stability of this joint is maintained by two ligaments that cross over inside the joint and are attached to the upper bone (the femur), and the lower bone (the tibia).

In the Labrador, these ligaments appear to be less robust than one would expect for a dog of this size, and, consequently, they can snap, in particular the anterior (cranial) ligament. This results in joint instability and immediate pain, and loss of weight-bearing by the dog.

Nonsurgical treatment is usually relatively ineffective. Painkillers decrease the discomfort but, because of the Labrador's nature, overuse of the joint is likely to occur, resulting in further injury. Modern surgical techniques can repair or replace the ligament, and, in the majority of cases, the function is soon restored without even a trace of lameness.

Unfortunately, because of the breed disposition, there is always the fear that, if one leg has been affected, subsequently the other one may suffer the same fate.

In particularly exuberant dogs, you might consider giving a good lead walk before they are allowed free for uncontrolled exercise, since rupture of the ligament often occurs when the dog is rapidly changing direction—something at which most young Labradors seem to excel, rushing here and there with complete abandon.

Although by no means exhaustive, these are the main conditions to which Labradors are particularly prone, in addition to the infectious conditions, diseases, and injuries that can unfortunately affect any dog.

A healthy, happy Labrador is a joy to share your life with.